MY SHEEP HAVE EARS

© Copyright 2015 by Cath Livesey

Published by 3DM Publishing
3dmpublishing.com

First Edition

First printing 2015

Printed in the United Kingdom

1 2 3 4 5 6 7 8 9 10 Printing/Year 25 24 23 22 21 20 19 18 17 16 15

Artwork & Illustrations: John Rainford

Layout & Design: Shaun Millward

ISBN: 978-0-9965300-3-3

Table of Contents

Acknowledgements   i

Foreword   iii

Part One: Hearing the Shepherd's Voice

Chapter 1:
Discovering God's Voice   3

Chapter 2:
Learning to Tune In   17

Chapter 3:
Hearing God for Others   35

Part Two: Prophets

Chapter 4:
The Ministry of Jesus   53

Chapter 5:
The Role of Prophets   67

Chapter 6:
A Pathway to Maturity   83

Part Three: Revelation

Chapter 7:

The Spirit of Truth and Revelation   99

Chapter 8:

The Revelation of the Trinity   111

Chapter 9:

Different Types of Revelation   121

Chapter 10:

What do we do with Revelation?   135

Part Four: The Bottom Line

Chapter 11:

Covenant   151

Chapter 12:

Kingdom   163

Chapter 13:

Doing Prophecy Well   179

Afterword   195

Acknowledgements

This book has very much been written within the family of 3DM Europe, so special thanks to Rich and Anna Robinson, Si Ford, Shaun and Joanna Millward, Pip Martin, Andrea Cheevers, Mark and Jacolien van den Steenhoven, Craig Millward, Sarah Burch, Nike Adebajo, John White and Jack Weaver. And thanks also to Joanna Dobson for your invaluable input.

Foreword

When I took over the leadership of St. Thomas' Church Philadelphia in 2004, I oversaw the subsequent joining together with another church in the city, King's Centre, to form what is now Network Church Sheffield. As these two churches joined together to form a single family across the two sites, I was aware of a significant number of people with real leadership gifts and skills who were still to step into leadership roles. I was also aware that the church had made an excellent start in learning to operate with a culture of missional discipleship and in learning to operate biblically with the spiritual gifts, but that there was also a way to go on the journey to maturity in these areas.

One of the leaders who emerged at this time was Cath Livesey. Cath is a woman of great integrity who is passionate about the Word of God and about the Holy Spirit. She has set herself to grow in the spiritual gifts and to help others to do the same, while keeping a firm hold on scripture and a grounded, common-sense approach to ministry.

I wanted the church to grow in sharpness and accuracy in the area of prophecy; the Bible tells us that the sheep hear the Shepherd's voice and that we should eagerly desire prophecy, and it felt as if we were ready to press into this more. I asked Cath to take responsibility for growing a team of people who could help the church in this respect, and also to develop a way to train members of the church to grow in their biblical understanding of prophecy, in their confidence in ministering to others and in their accuracy in hearing God's voice.

Cath has been responsible for building a culture of responsible, biblical prophecy in the church over a number of years now, where everyday Christians have learned to hear the still small voice of God with authenticity instead of hype; with accuracy and humility in equal measure. She has addressed the dangers of this kind of ministry, identifying ways to avoid manipulation or sensationalism and teaching people to operate in a way which edifies and builds up the body. As she has done this, an increasing number of other churches have asked her to come alongside them and help them to develop a similar culture in their own congregations.

Cath's ministry has been a huge blessing to me and to many churches over the years. My prayer is that through this book, it will also be a blessing to you. If you want to move on in hearing God but you also want to do so in a responsible and a thoroughly biblical way, you will find this book invaluable.

Rev Paul Maconochie - Executive Team Leader, 3DM USA

To St.John, Joanna, Kate and Isabel

With all my love

Part One

Hearing the Shepherd's Voice

Chapter 1

Discovering God's Voice

It had been a very busy and draining few weeks, and I was feeling ill with one of those winter viruses that are so hard to shake off. But I had managed to carve out a free morning from my schedule and the aim was simple: to re-connect with God.

If I'm honest I wasn't feeling too optimistic – sometimes even prayer seems an effort when we're over-tired and in a low mood. But I resisted the urge to simply go back to bed, and instead headed out to my beloved Peak District with the dog and a longing in my heart for the joy of God's presence.

It was a grey day in early December and for me it wasn't about finding God in the beauty of my surroundings. But as I engaged with the spiritual disciplines of thanksgiving and praise whilst tramping across Burbage Edge, I could start to sense the stress and sluggishness of the last few weeks slip away and once again I could begin to engage with the sweet fellowship of the Holy Spirit.

And then, as I sat on one of those huge slabs of gritstone that mark this particular landscape, it happened; but in such a quiet and everyday way that I almost missed its significance. God spoke to me. He spoke in answer to a question I'd just asked him; he spoke both in my surroundings but also deep in my heart. He spoke with clear reassurance but in the quietest of whispers. He spoke in the voice that over the years I have come to treasure more than anything else.

It wasn't an earth-shattering revelation. There were certainly no angels or visions of glory. But it was God's voice for sure, talking to me about something that mattered to me. And as I made my way back to the car my heart was filled with gratitude that he had given me ears to hear him; that this particular follower of Jesus had learnt how to hear the Good Shepherd's voice.

This is a book about prophecy and how a broad, multi-faceted, and biblical approach to prophetic gifts and ministry can edify and equip God's people to become more radical followers of Jesus and engage more effectively with the world around them. We will define and explain prophecy in later chapters of this book. But we're going to start by looking at what it actually means to hear God's voice for **ourselves**: how this should be a key aspect of our walk with the Lord, and how learning to listen to him is something we can all do.

What Does It Mean To Hear God's Voice?

The more I read the Bible the more I become convinced that an absolutely fundamental part of our spiritual inheritance as Christians is that we can learn to hear and identify the voice of God. I'm not talking about hearing God through the words of scripture, as precious and necessary as that is, but about hearing his 'now' words to us, words that speak directly into our current, specific reality; words that guide us every step of the way. I'm talking about his actual **voice**.

A few years ago a friend of mine said these words to me: *"I can never imagine being so close to God that I would actually hear him speak to me"*. And I guess there are plenty of Christians going around with that attitude: *Why would Almighty God want to speak to 'little old me'? I'm not good or holy enough. I'm no-one special.* But my personal testimony, as a normal and every day Christian, is that I have learnt how to hear God's voice. Yes, it's been quite a long and frustrating journey at times, and I've made *many* mistakes along the way, but I have learnt to hear the voice of my heavenly Father as he speaks to me. I've learnt what his voice sounds like and I've learnt how to trust and follow his voice, and I know there are millions of Christians around the world who have been on the same journey and share my testimony: *God speaks today!*

I want to be really clear here. I've never heard the audible voice of God; I don't hear his voice with my physical ears. When I talk about hearing God's voice I'm talking about hearing him speak to me in a spiritual, internal language. This is a language that is just as real as the spoken English that my friends and family communicate to me in, but one that has taken me longer to become acquainted with. Part of the journey for me in learning this language has been understanding that I am a spiritual being, and that God speaks to me in the language of the Spirit. It's a language of incredible depth and beauty; but a language that's so simple that a child can learn it.

I've heard God speak in the really big things, such as whom I was going to marry and when to sell our house; and I've heard him in the mundane, everyday and seemingly insignificant. I've heard him speak words of love, identity and comfort to me, as well as words of warning, correction and challenge. God's spoken voice has become my guide, my strength and my joy.

Again, I want to be really clear: throughout my life I have read, studied, and taught the Bible. I love the Bible and recognise it as the written word of God. It's an incredible book! But it was never intended to be the whole counsel of God – because God also speaks into our present reality through his voice into our hearts. As friends of God we have the immense privilege of being able to hear him both in the Bible **and** through his voice. We need both.

Biblical Promise

When we look at the Bible we clearly see that God is a communicating God. He communicates through creation, he communicates through the scriptures, he communicates through angels and all sorts of wonderful supernatural experiences. And he primarily chooses to communicate with his people through his voice. From Genesis to Revelation God is speaking.

He uses his voice to:

- create the universe
- reveal himself and his nature
- to call people into relationship with him
- to instruct, lead and guide

In fact it's quite hard to find a book in the Bible that doesn't at least have a reference to God's spoken word. The God that we love and worship is certainly not silent.

These verses from Isaiah 50:4-5 challenge us to pay close attention to the voice of God:

> *The Sovereign Lord has given me a well-instructed tongue, to know the word that sustains the weary. He wakens me morning by morning, wakens my ear to listen like one being instructed. The Sovereign Lord has opened my ears; I have not been rebellious, I have not turned away.*

Not only is God speaking to his people throughout the Bible, but the scriptures indicate that men and women were created to hear this voice clearly. The fact that God speaks and people hear is taken for granted in the Bible to the extent that the mechanism for this communication is never really explained. Instead time after time we read that *The Lord said to...*, and it is the subsequent obedience or disobedience to this voice that forms the basis for the biblical narrative.

One of the tragic aspects of the Old Testament story and its description of God's relationship with his covenant people is that as his people chose more and more to walk away from him, his voice became rarer.

Abraham was a man who recognised God's voice, responded in faith to God's voice, and obeyed God's instructions. God's intention for Abraham's descendants was that they would be a **nation of priests** (Exodus 19:6), walking so closely to the Lord that they would faithfully listen to him and represent him before all other nations. But at the critical moment at Mount Sinai they chose to hold back:

> *When the people saw the thunder and lightning and heard the trumpet and saw the mountain in smoke, they trembled with fear. They stayed at a distance and said to Moses, "Speak to us yourself and we will listen. But do not have God speak to us or we will die."*
> Exodus 20:18-19

Fear robbed them of the opportunity to enter into their role as priests; instead they chose to have Moses as their intermediary, who would hear God on their behalf. From that time the priestly and prophetic ministries were reserved for a select few, and as the story moves from patriarch to judge to king, God's voice came only on an occasional basis through the Prophets.

The good news for us is that under the new covenant the call to God's people to function as a kingdom of priests is renewed: we all have direct access to God, each believer has the ability to hear. Through the blood of Jesus we have come to another mountain, but this one is Mount Zion, the heavenly city of God (Hebrews 12:22-25), and we have the opportunity to respond with faith to the voice of God:

> *See to it that you do not refuse him who speaks.*
> Hebrews 12:25

Instead of a limited few, everyone is a priest and able to come directly into the presence of God. God's voice is available to all. To help us understand this covenantal truth, Jesus, the mediator of the new covenant, describes this new dynamic using the imagery of a shepherd and his sheep.

The Sheep Who Listen

In the middle of John's gospel we find a wonderfully clear and simple picture of what hearing God's voice is supposed to look like. In chapter 10 Jesus describes himself as the Good Shepherd who leads his sheep by his voice. In fact Jesus says four times in this chapter that his sheep know and listen to his voice.

Middle-eastern shepherds in those days led their sheep from the front (rather than driving them from behind) and the sheep followed because they recognised the voices of these shepherds. Jesus presents us with this wonderful imagery of himself as the Good Shepherd. A shepherd with a voice. A shepherd with sheep who have ears.

The sheep in John 10 are able to do three things:

- know the voice of the Good Shepherd
- listen to his voice
- follow **only** his voice

Jesus' promise is clear: he will be our faithful shepherd and we will know his voice to such an extent that we will be able to follow it. And as we seek to become better hearers of his voice, simple faith in this promise is going to be key for us.

Being a Disciple

In fact being able to hear the voice of the Good Shepherd is inherent to being a follower, a disciple, of Jesus. Discipleship is at the very heart of our Christian faith. The call on our lives is not simply to believe in Jesus but to **follow** him as disciples. And we can only consistently and effectively follow him if we learn to recognise his voice and respond with obedience.

What is a disciple? Disciples are people who are following Jesus – they have made that decision to follow him and to learn from him. In fact the New Testament word for disciple is the Greek word *mathetes* and it means 'learner'. The call on all of us as we seek to follow Jesus is to:

> Learn to **be** like Jesus, and learn to **do** what Jesus could do.

To be a disciple is to be constantly learning and looking to Jesus to hear what he wants us to do, and then to live it out. Disciples choose to listen and obey – to hear first and then step out in obedience and follow the Shepherd. This is the essence of discipleship.

As we choose to follow Jesus, he sets us this wonderful example: he chose to live his life on earth in close intimacy with his heavenly Father and to only do what he saw his Father doing (John 5:19). He also chose to be completely led by the Spirit. He prayed, retreated, listened – and then stepped out in obedience to the Holy Spirit. Jesus models for us a lifestyle of listening and then stepping out in faith so that we are always walking in step with the Father.

This principle of listening and then obeying is illustrated in the parable of the Wise and Foolish Builders at the end of the Sermon on the Mount (Matthew 7:24-27). Jesus compares the wise man that built his house on the rock with the foolish man who built his house on sand: when the wind and rains came we know which house was left standing. Jesus makes it clear that it's not enough to just **hear** his words, we also have to **act** on them:

> *"Therefore everyone who hears these words of mine and puts them into practice is like a wise man who built his house on the rock."*

Jesus uses this parable to reveal to his followers the two fundamental questions of discipleship:

What is God saying to you?

What are you going to do about it?

We will come back to this biblical principle of 'hear and obey' at various points in this book. It's as we intentionally embrace the discipline of these two questions that we will become life-long learners of Jesus. To follow in the footsteps of Jesus requires us to be people of faith and dependency, because hearing God is about having faith that he will speak, and then choosing to live in complete dependency on him: *I want to know how **You** want me to live.* Discipleship is choosing not to live from our own strength, but instead rely wholly on him.

A Listening Lifestyle

Intentionally living a listening lifestyle is fundamental to being a disciple. The Good Shepherd speaks in many different ways (we'll unpack many of these later on) – we simply have to learn to recognise his voice and to attune our hearts to his. He has given us ears to hear his voice – it's our responsibility as disciples to ensure our ears are attentive, not dulled.

As a disciple of Jesus Christ I want to have a listening lifestyle so that every step I take is shaped and guided by the voice of my Good Shepherd. I want to live a life where I closely follow in the footsteps of Jesus, and where every day I look to see what the Father is doing.

But how do I get there? Whenever we want to set in place a particular lifestyle – one that echoes that pattern of the kingdom – we need to start with **spiritual disciplines**, because discipline leads to habit, and habit leads to lifestyle:

Discipline ➤ Habit ➤ Lifestyle

As we intentionally choose to engage with disciplines, in time they become a habit, and habits in time become a lifestyle.

So what disciplines can we embrace that will set us up so that in time we are living a listening lifestyle?

1. The discipline of listening to God as we read his written word.
2. The discipline of listening to God as we pray.
3. The discipline of stepping back and listening to his voice every time we have a significant decision to make.
4. The discipline of listening to God as we go about our normal, everyday lives: doing the washing up, driving to work, mowing the lawn, walking the dog.
5. The discipline of listening to God in the midst of all our different relationships with people, so we hear his counsel in the words of our friends, and so we can speak as he would speak to others.

For some people a listening lifestyle comes easily and naturally – the Shepherd's voice is close and accessible, hearing flows unhindered. But for the majority of us it is something to be deliberately pursued. If you've grown up in a culture where hearing God's voice is rare and unexpected, then fully embracing a listening lifestyle is going to be a challenge. But it is something within the reach of every one of us. That is Jesus' promise to us. And when Jesus talked about the sheep hearing his voice he wasn't just talking about individual animals: the sheep hear best when they are part of a flock – *a community committed to listening*.

A Culture of 'Everyone Hears'

A healthy discipleship culture is not just one where we hear God as individuals, it's one where we hear him in the context of community and *together* we become good listeners of the Good Shepherd's voice. As we pursue a desire to hear God better it's important for us to belong to a family of disciples with a common commitment to hearing and obeying.

Whatever environment we are thinking about – whether it's our small group, missional community[1] or church – the culture that we want to see developed is one in which everyone is learning to listen.

A culture of 'everyone hears' and a community with ears attuned to the voice of the Shepherd doesn't mean everyone is a prophet, or everyone has 3D techni-coloured visions all the time. But it does mean that everyone can hear what God wants for their life and put it into practice. And it means that there is an expectation and confidence that God is going to speak.

What does a culture of 'everyone hears' look like? We'll unpack this question as we journey through this book, but our initial broad brush-strokes are:

- disciples living from the heart of God – secure in the **covenant** love that flows from the heart of their heavenly Father, and confident that it is the Father's intention to reveal his heart to them

- disciples who know how to **recognise and respond** to God's voice – who recognise the voice of the Shepherd in the midst of all the other distracting voices that clamour for their attention – and then wholeheartedly respond

- disciples allowing God's voice to **challenge and refine them** – so that God's voice becomes an active ingredient in shaping, refining and making them more like Jesus

As we've already seen, one of the key markers of a discipling culture (and therefore a listening culture) is people being asked the question on a regular basis: *"What is God saying to you and what are you going to do about it?"* It's vital that these two questions go together, because when God speaks into our lives he does so for a purpose. Every word he speaks to us has the power to make us

---

[1] Missional Communities are a group of 20-50 people forming an extended family who are on mission together.

more like Jesus, if we align our lives with it. He is committed to the transformation process necessary to produce disciples who can effectively do the works of the kingdom and change the world.

God's voice is not always cosy and comforting: it can be fire. We have to take his voice seriously. A culture of 'everyone hears' means being prepared to live our lives in such a way that God's voice will refine us – not just a surface engagement, but rather allowing his voice to go really deep and radically change us.

It's worth pointing out that even the simplest words of God have the power to utterly change us if we pause long enough to fully engage with them. Even the most simple and comforting word from the heart of the Father can and should change us. Hearing him speak the words, *"I love you,"* can be refining and transformative, as we choose to take this truth deep into ourselves and allow it to shape our very being. Every word that the Lord speaks to us can profoundly shape us if we want it to and if we decide to actively step out in faith on it. If we are going to allow God's voice to challenge and refine us then it's about giving space, time and energy to the process of hearing him and allowing his words to be fully absorbed. And we must do this in our church communities as well as in our own individual walk with God.

Only this morning during our prayer session I shared with the 3DM Europe team a word of encouragement that I believed the Lord had given me: God gave me a picture of us as a team standing behind Jesus. And Jesus was an incredible warrior, twice the size of us, in dazzling armour, who was fighting our battles with great energy and focus. Is this a nice little word of encouragement that stays with us for a few minutes and is then forgotten? Or do we pause long enough to feel the full weight of the revelation, let it shape our thinking all day long, and see the potential it has to change us *if* we fully engage with it?

However God speaks – however we hear his voice – we need to ask ourselves, *"Am I hearing and obeying Jesus?"* Remember that you are one of Jesus' sheep and he wants to lead you by his voice.

To end this chapter on listening to God I'd like to share with you a couple of stories from people I know well who have learnt how to hear and recognise the voice of the Good Shepherd. First of all, my friend Di:

Sheffield, early September 2006: I don't remember where I'd arrived home from, but to this day getting out of the car is etched in my memory. With one foot still in the car and one on solid ground, I heard God speak. "This time next year you'll be in a very different place." It wasn't an audible voice but I knew it was God, just as I knew when he spoke to me in dreams before I was a Christian. How do you describe the voice of God? For me, in this instance, it was an interruption to my train of thoughts, a quiet but determined idea that arrested my heart and captured my attention.

But what did he mean? I've had a long-standing connection with Germany and so assumed that within a year I'd be in that country, or maybe God was speaking of a different place in spiritual terms. What I could not have imagined is that a year later I would be living in Perth, Australia, the most isolated capital in the world.

I left the car, went home, dutifully recorded the event in my journal and got on with whatever was happening that evening, not really thinking too much about it. And that was that, until late January 2007.

I was helping at a healing retreat for young adults, and it was here that God chose to get my attention. He spoke to me directly through scripture and prophetic pictures, as well as through prophecies from other people. This was not what the weekend was supposed to be about: I was there to serve. However, by the end of the weekend, I knew that God was saying it was time to get ready to go. Finally, in the last worship time, I asked God, "OK, where're we going?" "To the ends of the earth," came the response. "And where might that be?" I enquired. "Australia," came the reply.

I knew it was God. At the time this particular country was not even on my radar, not least because I had an intense fear of flying and knew far too many people who had 'done

Australia'. After much internal turmoil I spoke to a close friend about what I felt God was saying. I was so settled in Sheffield, I was secretly hoping that she'd say I was crazy and should stay. She didn't. Nor did my wise leaders when I spoke to them. So it was time to sit with my trusted leaders and friends to plan. How would God lead me, a single woman, across the globe when it seems that the minimum unit in the kingdom is two? I knew nothing about Australia, and wasn't sure that I knew anyone there. As a member of The Order of Mission[2], it made sense to travel to be with other members in Australia and a few emails later, Malcolm and Cheryl Potts invited me to come join them in Perth.

So this is how, on the 1st August 2007, I arrived somewhat dishevelled and shell-shocked at Perth International Airport. I got on the plane with a sense – developed and processed over time – that God was sending me to share with others what he had invested in me, like a bee pollinating plants. I also felt that God was speaking of Australia as my Promised Land and that I needed to come here to grow into the person he's called me to be. I thought I'd be away from Sheffield for a year, spending three months in different places before returning home. I also got on the plane telling God that I'd do anything but teach. Well, I've been here seven years now and have been teaching in schools for most of that time. I'm also an Australian citizen now. Sharing what God had invested in me was just the beginning and I'm not sure that if I'd known I was leaving the UK forever, I'd have been able to get on the plane. The last seven years have been incredibly eventful in both exciting and challenging ways. What has enabled me to persevere in the challenging times has been the deep conviction that this is where God wants me to be. Because I processed with others what I felt God was saying, these trusted friends have been able to reassure me that I'm on God's path, even when everything within me and around me might be suggesting that I wasn't. As I write this, I am preparing to follow God's call once again,

---

[2] The Order of Mission is an apostolic mission order within the global Anglican Communion

this time to Tasmania. The way God has spoken has been different this time, but the relational process of discernment has remained the same.

Here's a story from my friend Dirk who is someone who has learnt that listening to God about our work situations can be very fruitful.

I am an engineer and a few years ago I was a technical manager responsible for developing new processes and equipment. My company had sold a major new project to a client in Austria. I was the guy who had the responsibility to start up this new factory and make the whole process work for our clients.

We had tested the new process in our works in Sheffield but when we started up the new machines at our customer's site, the critical part, the heart of the machine, simply couldn't be made to work at all. My colleagues and I tried absolutely everything humanly possible to make it work but after weeks and months of tests, trials and experiments it became clear that nothing we did was making it work properly.

I spent many weeks out there in Austria trying ever more desperately to make this plant work but nothing overcame the problems we encountered. To make things worse, back home our company was having a terrible time at the height of the 2008/9 global recession and we had to lay off half of our production staff. The customer in Austria was understandably extremely unhappy and started threatening us with a lawsuit because the plant he bought was quite obviously not working. If the company had taken us to court it would have been the end of our business since there was absolutely no way that we could have paid the money back that this customer had paid us.

At that point and in absolute desperation I sought the Lord for a solution. I have never been somebody who has had lots of amazing prophetic pictures or visions, but what happened next is something I will never forget.

I was on a train on my way to visit the component

manufacturer of the machine part that was the source of all my troubles, and God suddenly spoke to me through a bright picture in my mind. It was a picture of a cross. To be honest my first reaction was, "Great, thanks God, yes I know that all I need is Christ and his Cross, but really, what has that got to do with my situation..." But then I scribbled a cross on my notepaper and started to sketch. By the time that I arrived in France for the meeting, I had finally figured out what the vision was all about. The vision led me to design an entirely new concept for this failing component, and yes, you guessed it, it was in the shape of a cross. I asked the supplier if they were able to make such a 'complicated' component and I explained only that this was a new completely untested idea that I wanted them to try and make.

When I returned from this meeting to the UK my boss laughed about this idea and he thought that this would have pretty much no chance of working. Since we were so desperate for a solution he however agreed that we should give it a go, but insisted that we should continue with our improvement work on the more conventional component design in parallel. To cut a long story short, the conventional technology continued to fail every time we tried a newer improved design, and the new 'cross technology' turned out to work miraculously well. Not only did this component make the plant work properly, it also made it perform far better than any other comparable technology out there in the market. The customer was highly delighted and it made him a lot of money by helping him to make his products much more cheaply. The success of this plant, or rather the non-failure of this whole project, certainly turned my company back from the brink and saved it from going under. Since then the company has more than tripled in size and continues to have good prospects for the future. It has done wonders for my faith as well, as I realise that God is interested in my work life and can speak powerfully into any situation. I now pray more regularly for my job as well ....

Chapter 2

Learning to Tune In

In the first chapter we looked at why it's so important that disciples of Jesus can hear him speak to them. In this chapter we are going to look at how we can all learn to tune in to his voice. God speaks sovereignly – we cannot conjure up his voice or force him to speak to us; but we can position ourselves in such a way so that when he speaks we can hear him.

Over the years I've taught many different people how to hear God's voice, which has been a tremendous joy and privilege. But in doing this I've met a number of individuals who find it really hard; for all sorts of reasons there seem to be huge blocks that get in the way and prevent them from hearing. Some sheep seem to be pretty deaf.

I guess I've learnt two things from working with the hard of hearing:

1. Everyone can (eventually) learn to hear God's voice: there are no permanently deaf sheep in God's flock.
2. The battleground is almost always the mind.

The key to unblocking ears is the Bible: taking hold of biblical truth and allowing scripture to transform our minds. The enemy of the sheep is constantly waging war against our minds – in order to defeat him we have to actively and intentionally choose to walk in truth and faith.

For a deaf sheep to become a hearing sheep it has to **change its mind**.

The Bible has a word for this, *metanoia*, which we usually translate as 'repent'. The word 'repent' can often have negative associations with messages of condemnation without grace, but the essence of *metanoia* is to change your way of thinking, to embrace a new mindset, and allow this change to impact your lifestyle and behaviour. It's about adopting a new way of thinking which in turn becomes a new way of living; re-aligning our lives (both internal and external) so that they are in rhythm with Jesus.

To tune in – to hear the Shepherd's voice – we have to win the battle of the mindset. A mindset is a pattern of thought, an established set of assumptions, that incentivises and shapes our behaviours and choices. The problem for many of us is that we have mindsets that stand in opposition to us hearing the voice of God. Not only that, we are probably not even aware just how deceptive and immovable some of these mindsets can be.

Those of us who live in the 'West' find ourselves in a culture that all too often idolises the intellect and elevates rationalism and secularism above all other paradigms. The emphasis is always on reason and scepticism, and this has done much to shape our mindsets to an extent that they can systematically hinder us from comprehending the language of the Spirit. (Later on in the chapter we'll look at how rationalism can act as a specific block to hearing God.)

Now there is nothing fundamentally wrong with intellectual thought, as long as it doesn't become an idol. I'm someone who loves science and generally has quite a logical and rational approach to life – it's the way God has made me. But I know that for me to fully engage with the kingdom of God I have to surrender my intellect to the Lord and allow him to refine my thought processes. And where my mindset has not been in alignment with his truth – if my thought life has been in opposition to the truth of the gospel – I've had to repent. I've changed my way of thinking. *I've surrendered my mind to the Lordship of Christ*.

Over the years I've frequently come back to the wisdom of Proverbs 3:5-6:

> *Trust in the Lord with all your heart and lean not on your*

own understanding; in all your ways submit to him, and he will make your paths straight.

As we seek to embrace a mindset that will allow us to fully engage with the voice of God, the first step is actively choosing not to lean on our human understanding, and instead submit to a godly way of thinking that simply trusts and believes that God speaks to his people.

One of my Danish friends, Anders, was recently telling me how he had been brought up to believe that God didn't speak today – that was his mindset:

"God isn't going to speak to me; I can't hear his voice; people in the Bible heard the voice of God but that doesn't happen any more."

But when Anders moved to a church with a different approach, people started regularly asking him the question, *"What is God saying to you today?"* At first Anders' response was based on his analysis of the sermon. But as people kept asking him the same question he started to consider the possibility that he might be able to hear God speak to him personally. In this new environment Anders' mind began to change. As his mind changed he started actively listening for God and found a relational God who was really speaking to him. The new mindset opened up a whole new dimension of his faith and today Anders hears God with great clarity.

Romans 12:2 promises us that if we choose to surrender our worldly patterns of thinking, our minds can be renewed:

> *Do not conform to the pattern of this world, but be transformed by the renewing of your mind. Then you will be able to test and approve what God's will is -- his good, pleasing and perfect will.*

We can 'renew our minds' in such a way that hearing God's voice becomes a natural, everyday occurrence. And even if tuning in to his voice is something that we're used to, it's good to do a regular 'health check' to ensure that the flow of revelation remains pure and unhindered.

We were designed and created to hear God's voice – it's in the blueprint. We just need to ensure that our thinking is in line with this truth.

Changing the Way We Think

As I've led many people through the journey from being a deaf sheep to becoming a fully hearing sheep, these four steps have been key in helping them change the way they think:

1. Know who you are

Do you **really** know who you are? The first step in changing our minds is to really get to grips with our identity as God's children. As followers of Jesus we are now part of God's family and the eternal and everlasting God is our heavenly Father. God is love, and the Bible has so much to teach us about the goodness, kindness and generosity of our perfect heavenly Dad.

And fathers like talking to their kids.

The problem is that so many of us struggle to live in the truth of our spiritual adoption. We may know in our heads that God is our Father, but still find ourselves reacting to situations as a fatherless orphan. We've been adopted as sons and daughters, but some of us still have a tendency to think and behave as orphans. Orphans feel they have to fight for everything; they find their identity in other sources; they strive for recognition and affirmation, trying to earn God's favour:

If I try harder, God will be pleased with me and he might even speak to me.

Whereas sons and daughters know they have a loving and affirming Father and live from a place of security, peace, significance, identity:

Of course I can hear God speak to me – I'm his beloved child and he delights to speak to me.

Learning to think like a son or daughter of our perfect heavenly Father is absolutely key in learning how to tune in to God's voice. When we really know to the depths of our being that we are children of a loving Father who wants the very best for us and who desires to pour out his unending love upon us, it profoundly changes our outlook on life. Knowing, and living out, our true identity releases us into hearing God, because it produces a mindset that is aligned with the truth that our Father speaks to his children.

2. Believe you will hear

As our thoughts become more aligned with the truth of our identity we can then begin to intentionally embrace a mindset of faith, a mindset that believes that we will indeed be able to hear God's voice.

Throughout the gospels we see that faith was the response Jesus was always looking for in people, and as we set out to follow him today he is not content to leave us in a place of little faith. Jesus' intention for us is that through the process of discipleship our minds become aligned with his and we become people whose default thinking pattern is, *"I can hear God"* – because he promised us that his sheep hear his voice. Interestingly, most children find it easy to hear God's voice, because they tend to have a more simple and uncluttered faith.

Jesus wants us to take his words seriously and allow them to create expectation and build faith. At the end of the day we all have a choice: we can choose to believe that God wants to speak to us and that we can hear him, or not. Once we've made the decision to believe the words of Jesus then we can start to meditate on and feed our souls with biblical truth. Memorising key scripture is always a good idea:

- *My sheep listen to my voice; I know them, and they follow me.* John 10:27
- *The Spirit will receive from me what he will make known to you.* John 16:15
- *What no eye has seen, what no ear has heard ... these are the things God has revealed to us by his Spirit.* 1 Corinthians 2:9-10
- *But we have the mind of Christ.* 1 Corinthians 2:16
- *And God raised us up with Christ and seated us with him in the heavenly realms in Christ Jesus.* Ephesians 2:6

Jesus is our Good Shepherd and he promises that we will hear his voice. He does not hold back from revealing his thoughts to us, and desires to show us the secret wisdom of his kingdom as we journey with him. We carry the Spirit of Almighty God in us and are seated in the heavenly realms with Jesus Christ. We're supernatural people!

We need to embrace the biblical mindset that we are spiritual beings who can perceive the kingdom of God and tune in to the voice of God. Let's have faith to believe that we can hear him.

3. Recognise all the 'normal' everyday ways God does speak to us and be thankful

Hearing the voice of God does not have to involve

- a burning bush
- an angel of the Lord
- a 3-D technicolor vision with added surround-sound

I hope that doesn't disappoint you. Because most of the time God speaks in fairly normal and everyday ways, to normal and everyday people. A key part of learning to tune in to his voice is recognising that God is already speaking – we're just not always very good at appreciating and acknowledging it.

Some of these 'normal and everyday' ways that God speaks to us are:

- through our conscience
- through a sense of peace
- through circumstances
- through the counsel of others
- through creation

And as we pause long enough to recognise God's voice as it manifests itself around us, then the way we think about God's voice is going to change. **Thanksgiving** is going to play an important role.

In fact if you would describe yourself as someone who really struggles to hear God's voice I would strongly recommend that you spend some time simply giving thanks for all the ways he has already spoken to you. All those times he has spoken to you through the Bible; the times he has guided you through a sense of peace; the times he has brought you counsel through the words of a wise friend; the times you have had a sudden clarity about a decision being made.

Thanksgiving is always such a great place to start in this journey of pursuing the voice of God. We need to change the way we think and be expectant that he will speak to us using the everyday texture of our lives. Don't despise the day of small things (Zechariah 4:10).

4. Understand that we all hear God in different ways

This simple truth can actually be incredibly liberating when we realise that God has made us as unique individuals and speaks to each of us in different ways.

Interestingly, although the Bible is full of stories about people hearing God, it doesn't tend to go into details about exactly what the experience was like for the particular individual. I suspect that if we could interview Moses, Elijah and the rest, we would discover that they encountered and discerned the voice of God in and through a variety of different processes and practices. My experience as I've talked to many people about hearing God, is that different people hear God in different ways, and these are often reflected in our different personalities and character traits. I've also discovered that the most conducive environment or context for hearing God differs from person to person.

It's important to identify the way you primarily hear God speak – how you receive revelation. It's probably not the same as the person sitting next to you. There is certainly a danger of looking at people who perhaps have a more visible prophetic ministry and thinking that's the only way to do it: *"I've got to hear God like they hear God."* Such conjecture can hold us back from hearing God for ourselves in the particular language that God uses to talk to us.

God has made me a very visual person. I love art and design and gain a tremendous amount of pleasure from looking at things. And the primary way God speaks to me is through simple prophetic pictures in my mind. In terms of the most conductive context for me, over the years I've often heard God most easily in times of worship – worship is a great environment for me to engage with God's voice. It's very different for my husband, though. He's not at all visual (and rarely notices if I've had my hair cut or painted a room in the house!) But God has made him to be someone with a very conceptual mind who loves new ideas. God speaks to him in the midst of these new ideas as he has learnt to recognise which of them are from God through a deep sense of 'knowing'. And he finds that prayer walking is the best environment to clearly hear God, because the simple activity of walking helps to minimise the distractions that a very creative mind can generate.

I love talking to people and finding out about the particular languages God uses to speak to them. And I love the dimension differing personalities brings to the spectrum of hearing God. Here are a couple of examples from two of my colleagues at 3DM Europe:

> As an introvert the context that is important to me is having space to myself on my own. Quite often I will be reading the Bible and God will take me off into a rabbit hole. I'll read a scripture and ask God what he's saying. Often a particular sentence or a word or phrase will stick out to me. Then I might be reminded of another passage that relates to the first one, and maybe a few others after that and a certain theme will arise from what I have read.
>
> Another way I hear from God is if, say, I have had a conversation with someone and want to know what God is saying, I'll sit on my own for five minutes afterwards and ask God what was significant about that conversation, and what I need to remember. Whatever of that conversation then comes to mind or feels significant is what I believe God is saying about it.
>
> When I get a prophetic word from God which I feel needs to be shared with someone, I basically start getting this download of language. As an introvert I can often struggle with turning my internal thoughts into spoken language.

However, when I get a prophetic word, God gives me this stream of language that I have to quickly write down. I won't have thought about it or have internally processed it as I do with all of my thoughts. I also don't have to try at all to formulate the language; the prophetic word just seems to go through me as if I'm listening to someone else say it.

Simon

I hear from God in a variety of ways. I think being an active person, with an active body and an active imagination, I generally struggle to sit still. So I generally do something around activity and nature. Going out for a walk or run helps me to have my body active but my mind at rest. Ironing is also a great place to hear God as it keeps my body active but gives my mind space to listen. So with a bit of worship music on I might walk, run or iron so that I'm able to mentally settle while I'm physically active.

Another great environment for me to hear God is sitting in a coffee shop by myself, because I like the noise and people around me but at the same time it gives me space to tune into his voice.

The way I actually hear God varies. One way is through the Bible – I just read about different characters and or different books and simply reflect on them, listening to what God says to me through that. I also like to journal, so having a conversation with the Lord through writing. As an extrovert, writing out what I think helps me to feel like I'm having a two-way conversation with the Holy Spirit. I also hear God in silence: the discipline of silence and stopping. Perhaps staring out the window or looking at a painting in a coffee shop. Just stopping and stilling my mind, listening and seeing what pops into my head or what I think of. Then I just journal that and let that train of thought of consciousness or unconsciousness disappear into what I think God is saying to me.

In terms of my leadership role, I'm always asking God, "What are you saying to me about or for this person, or for this situation?" I do that as a discipline before I go into meetings or when I find myself in conversation so that I don't drift but make an active decision to listen. I'm the sort of person who has 101 words and ideas for every solution and circumstance, so it's important that I actively make myself listen to God. Often I'll have two or three trains of thought in conversation, so I settle on the one that I have a sense of peace about, which is what God is saying or what I feel God is calling us to do.

Rich

The encouragement is to discover and explore the unique way God has made you, and then find his voice in the midst of that.

Blocks, Interference and Filters

We've looked at how we can change the way we think, and how powerful the right mindset can be in helping us tune in to God's voice. As we further unpack the paradigm of good or bad mindsets, it can be very helpful to think in terms of the **specific hindrances** that stop us clearly hearing the voice of the Good Shepherd. We need to identify and challenge all the 'stuff' that gets in the way. Three simple visual pictures may help here:

A block in the way : a barrier that comes between God's voice and us.

Other voices : picture the scenario of sitting in a noisy pub or cafe, trying to listen to a friend, with many other voices that are fighting for your attention. These create so much interference and distraction that it becomes hard to hear what your friend is saying.

A filter that changes : Photographers use filters to affect the
or distorts the clear way light enters the camera. Some filters
picture dramatically alter the quality of the image
produced, others have a much more
subtle effect. A filter doesn't block the
light, but it does distort it.

These hindrances often fit under the umbrella term of 'mindset', but what we are talking about here are **specific and personalised thought-patterns or emotions** that need to be identified so that we can deal with them.

In many ways the journey towards hearing God better is all about removing things; removing the barriers and obstructions that we have unwittingly accumulated over time. It's also about choosing what to listen to – refocusing our attention away from every clamouring voice that would distract us from God's voice. I would really encourage you to actively engage with this process. Too many of us readily accept poor hearing and simply acquiesce to the presence of deterrents that shut out the voice of God. For the vast majority of us there will be something in our lives that is stopping us from hearing as clearly as we could. Some of the most common blocks, interferences and filters are:

- false beliefs
- rationalism
- fear
- shame
- our agendas

Let's look at each of these in more detail.

1. False beliefs

These are usually the specific beliefs that, *"God never speaks to me,"* or, *"I can't hear God"*. These can be very loud voices in our minds, and have their origins in lies: either lies that have been told to us, or lies that we've told ourselves. Perhaps we've had experiences in the past that make it very easy to listen to this particular voice. Perhaps we've stepped out in the prophetic in the past, got it wrong, or not been listened to, and we end up speaking the lie over ourselves that we can't hear God; we vow never to try it again. Or perhaps other people tell us that what we think is God's voice is only our own imagination. Lies like this can have devastating consequences in the life of a disciple trying to follow Jesus.

False beliefs have to be discerned and confronted. We have to be ruthless with ourselves and examine our thought patterns. We have to welcome both the Holy Spirit and fellow Christians to bring godly challenge to our belief systems. If we find any aspect of our thinking that is not in alignment with all that God has for us, then we need to repent of believing a lie, and set our minds on truth, taking hold of the promise of the Good Shepherd.

2. Rationalism

Rationalism can act as a significant block to us hearing God's voice when we lean too much on our own understanding and worldly wisdom, particularly at the moment of initially discerning his revelation. As I've said earlier, there is nothing inherently wrong with rationalism as an approach to understanding the world around us, but an over-emphasis on reason in our journey of faith and hearing God is going to hinder us.

This is a block I have had to overcome in my own walk with Jesus, because my analytical mind has a tendency to question everything and shout out, *"That can't be God," "That doesn't make sense,"* as soon as revelation appears. The danger is that rationalism causes us to dismiss God's voice the moment it appears, because it makes no sense to us. We have to realise that hearing God is spiritual, not logical. I've had to learn to respond to revelation with my spirit rather than my mind, and rely much more on faith rather than logic.

3. Fear

There are, unfortunately, many fears that block, distort or interfere with our receptivity to God's voice. For some people the voice of fear resounds so loudly that it drowns out everything else:

- fear of getting it wrong

- fear of the unknown
- fear of having the wrong motives
- fear of deception – frightened that the enemy is going to speak to us rather than God

There was a time a few years ago when I realised that a particular fear was acting as a huge block to me hearing God's voice: it was the fear that if I properly listened to him he would tell me to do something that I didn't want to do – like sell all my belongings and go off to be a missionary. So every time I tried to approach him and listen to what he wanted to say to me, the fear popped up and blocked the flow of revelation.

Of course most fears are rooted in lies, and the lie that I was entertaining was that God was a strict father who was never quite satisfied with me and wanted me to be miserable. Thankfully once I realised that this was a lie I was able to repent of believing it – and the block disappeared.

4. Shame

Shame gets in the way of us hearing God because it causes us to withdraw from his presence out of a feeling of unworthiness. Like fear, shame is rooted in lies, and it's all too easy for the voice of shame to crowd out the voice of God. Paying attention to the lying voice that says, *"I'm not good enough to hear God; I've messed up too many times; I'm pretty useless,"* is going to make it very hard for us to hear the sweet voice of Jesus.

5. Our agendas

When it comes to our personal agendas my observation is that they function more as filters rather than blocks. They allow quite a lot of revelation to come through to us, but will always subtly change and distort it. If we're really serious about becoming a sheep with excellent hearing then there is only one thing we can do with our agendas: surrender them. Lay them on the altar. Nail them to the Cross.

The problem is that they have the habit of being fairly elusive and even masquerading as kingdom business. We need to become aware of these subtle 'filters' that affect the clarity of our hearing:

- our opinions
- our agendas for other people
- wanting to impress/people pleasing
- our desires
- apathy
- our theology

(You may be surprised to see theology on the list, but it's all too easy to filter Spirit-breathed revelation through our particular theological standpoint.)

When we hold such agendas in overly high esteem they actually become idols in our hearts, and we are in danger of mistaking the voice of our idols for God's voice. Even when we feel confident in our ability to hear God we still have to beware the danger of such agendas creeping in. For example, if we are asking God about a particular issue it's important to examine our hearts carefully first to ensure that we are *seeking first his kingdom and his righteousness* (Matthew 6:33). As we actively lay down our personal agendas his voice will resound in our hearts with greater clarity.

Removing the Blocks

How do we tackle these specific blocks, interferences and filters that are robbing us of our ability to tune in to God's voice? The great news is that God is so committed to us hearing him that once we make a decision to work with him on removing these hindrances he will give us all the grace we need.

The first step is **recognising** the block, and of course we can be regularly praying that the Lord would show us anything that is getting in the way of us hearing him. If you are struggling to tune in to his voice then I would really encourage you to spend some time asking God to show you what the problem is and where it has come from. There may very well be a cost to you doing this – God is so committed to our spiritual growth that when we ask him questions like that he will often come to prune away the overgrowth and dead wood, and we need to surrender to his process. But it's worth it! And it's also important to involve other people – those you trust – who can often have a more objective view of what the hindrances may be. This is particularly the case with our agendas: when we hear and process revelation in the context of community then we are less likely to be affected by our agendas, because other people will be able to spot them.

Once we have identified the block or interference the next question is how we can remove it. Sometimes the key is **forgiveness**: if the words or actions of another person have resulted in something hindering us hearing God, then we have to choose to forgive them. Sometimes we have to forgive ourselves for acquiescing to the presence of the block.

The next step is laid out clearly in scripture and takes us back to the issue of mindsets. This is the biblical process of '**repent and believe**', an incredibly useful framework for dealing with blocks and hindrances:

> *"The time has come, the kingdom of God has come near. Repent and believe the good news"*
> Mark 1:15

> *"As for everyone who comes to me and hears my words and puts them into practice, I will show you what they are like. They are like a man building a house, who dug down deep and laid the foundation on rock."*
> Luke 6:47-48

> *Faith by itself, if it is not accompanied by action, is dead.*
> James 2:17

There is a very simple, but profound, principle that Jesus is talking about here: it's the principle of not just hearing truth, but embracing and **living out** that truth. Hear, and then obey.

Repent: as we saw at the beginning of the chapter, *metanoia* means to change our mind. This is about hearing and embracing God's truth; and using God's truth to change our mindsets.

We choose to no longer agree with the block, whether it's fear, unbelief or something else, laying it down at the foot of the cross, and trusting that Jesus has done all that is necessary to deal with it.

Believe: what we are talking about here is a substantive display of belief, so that we actually live the truth: the word is made flesh in our lives. It's about living out the new mindset by changing our behaviour or lifestyle. We allow the new way of thinking to affect our outward actions.

So for example, if unbelief has acted as a big block that stops you hearing God's voice, 'Repent' will mean choosing to take hold of the words of Jesus in John 10 that the sheep hear the Shepherd's voice; 'Believe' will mean that you start to *act on this truth*, intentionally living in an opposite spirit to the block, so that your behaviour is no longer defined by it. You will actively start listening to God; you will find people to practice prophesying over in a safe environment; you will regularly journal what you think God is saying to you. Basically you start to act as someone who can hear God easily.

The process of changing the way we think – the process of repentance – is an *internal one*. As I said at the beginning of this chapter, the battleground is first and foremost the mind. But to see real breakthrough we need to see *external* change that flows from the internal shift. True faith is seen in action.

Again, let me emphasise the importance of community in this process. We can't do it by ourselves! We cannot engage with the process of 'repent and believe' in isolation – we need to involve other people. Having the opportunity to reflect on, and discuss, our *metanoia* with those who are walking closely with us maximises the effectiveness of the process. It enables us to make the right decisions about the things we need to repent of, and ensures we can be accountable about the actions we take.

Changing the way we think is not a quick fix, but if we are daily choosing God's voice over all the others, then we can walk in this truth:

We demolish arguments and every pretension that sets

itself up against the knowledge of God, and we take captive every thought to make it obedient to Christ.
2 Corinthians 10:5.

We can be disciples who learn to embrace a godly mindset, who learn to tune out all the other distractions and interference, and who learn to tune in to his wonderful voice.

Learning to Listen

So how do you actually do it? How do you actually start to listen to God's voice? As long as you are content with taking small steps, and maintain thankfulness for every little breakthrough, then you can actively pursue revelation, knowing there is no shame in wearing 'L' plates for a season.

Here are some simple steps to tuning in. I use these exercises frequently, both when I'm teaching others how to tune in to God's voice, and also when I have time alone with God. The more we engage with this discipline, the more natural it will become. I have found Mark and Patti Virkler's teaching helpful [particularly their book *How to Hear God's Voice* (Destiny Image Publishers, 2013)] and have adapted their approach.

This is quite a systematic exercise, and as you are learning to tune into God's voice I suggest you approach it as you would any other training regime and commit some quality time to it.

1. Start in a place of thanksgiving and praise. Psalm 100 tells us that we enter into the Lord's presence through thanksgiving and praise. So spend some time giving thanks for all the blessings God has poured into your life, and then engage in praising him for who he is.

2. Rest in the Father's love. Remind yourself of your covenant identity as his beloved child. Enjoy being still in his presence, receiving his peace and knowing that the Father delights to speak to you.

3. Fix your thoughts and imagination on Jesus. Meditate a while on some of his names (e.g. Light of the World; Saviour; Bread of Life). Contemplate the visual descriptions we have of him in

scripture (e.g. Revelation 1: 12-18). Allow worship of Jesus to fill your heart and delight in him.

4. Welcome the presence of the Holy Spirit. Spend some time honouring him as the Spirit of Truth. Lay down your agendas before him and surrender to his leading.

5. Ask him to speak. Remember that God speaks in many different ways. So you may find that a fleeting image pops into your head, or the name of a friend, or a verse from the Bible. It may be something as simple as a sense of peace or love. Just go with it; don't dismiss it. Write it down and give thanks.

Chapter 3

Hearing God for Others

We've spent the first two chapters looking at how the sheep can learn to hear the voice of the Good Shepherd, and done this largely from the perspective of the individual, and his or her journey of learning to tune in. We're now going to start looking beyond individual sheep and consider how God's people can hear his voice in the context of community. What does a listening church look like? How do we move from hearing God for ourselves to **hearing God for others**?

Community is the crucial lens through which we must always view prophetic gifts, and as we look at the New Testament model of prophecy we see that its true home is a healthy, thriving community of God's people. Prophecy is not designed to exist in a vacuum.

What is Prophecy?

In many ways it's hard to come up with a simple definition of prophecy, but at its most basic level prophecy is about hearing God for other people.

When we look at the Bible we see that prophecy involves the process by which the thoughts and intentions of God are communicated to his people via a human vessel. Its origins are not human understanding and reasoning, but divine revelation:

> *For prophecy never had its origin in the human will* [we can't make it happen!]*, but prophets, though human, spoke from God as they were carried along by the Holy Spirit.*
> 2 Peter 1:21

Prophecy is supernatural. It is not of the earthly, physical realm. It is not something we can analyse and rationalise. It is the divine omniscience touching our spirits. No wonder human vocabulary struggles to encompass and fully express the depth and breadth of that connection.

When we examine the call of Jeremiah in the Old Testament we see prophecy in the context of someone being called to speak on behalf of God:

> *Then the Lord reached out his hand and touched my mouth and said to me, "Now, I have put my words in your mouth".* Jeremiah 1:9

– which is a classic description of the relationship between God and his prophet. Jeremiah becomes the vessel chosen to carry the words of God to his people. His role is to be God's mouthpiece.

In the New Testament the Greek word translated 'to prophesy' is *propheteuo* which is used in the Bible to mean *to speak forth by divine inspiration; to declare a thing that can only be known by divine revelation*. It signifies the speaking forth of the mind or counsel of God. God's thoughts are not man's thoughts (Isaiah 55:8), but through the medium of prophecy we gain a certain kind of access to God's way of thinking. Though, as Paul's great hymn to love in 1 Corinthians reminds us, this side of heaven it will always be *as a poor reflection in a mirror.*

Here are three examples from the New Testament of prophecy in action in the lives of believers:

| Through the prophetic ministry of Agabus God brings warning to the believers of a future famine. They take this prophecy seriously and act accordingly. | *During this time some prophets came down from Jerusalem to Antioch. One of them, named Agabus, stood up and through the Spirit predicted that a severe famine would spread over the entire Roman world. (This happened during the reign of Claudius.) The disciples, as each one was able, decided to provide help for the brothers and sisters living in Judea. This they did, sending their gift to the elders by Barnabas and Saul.* Acts 11:27-30 |

At a key moment in Acts God gives a clear word of direction. This prophecy shaped the missional strategy of the early church.	*While they were worshiping the Lord and fasting, the Holy Spirit said, "Set apart for me Barnabas and Saul for the work to which I have called them."* Acts 13:2
Prophecies had revealed God's call on Timothy's life, and at a later point Paul urges him to go back to them and gain strength from recalling them.	*Timothy, my son, I am giving you this command in keeping with the prophecies once made about you, so that by recalling them you may fight the battle well.* 1 Timothy 1:18

A really simply way to understand prophecy is to use this definition:

**Prophecy is hearing God speak,
and repeating what he says.**

So when we engage with prophecy there are two key elements: firstly hearing what God is saying, and then making it known to others. The prophetic is concerned with making known the heart, mind and intention of God.

Revelation : from God to person

Communication : from person to person

And of course communication does not always have to involve words. We can be prophetic through our actions, through the way we love and care for people, through standing up for righteousness and justice. Prophecy doesn't always have to involve speaking something out; what's key is that we are revealing God's heart to people.

Prophecy comes in many different expressions and sizes. I've delivered dynamic prophecies to crowds of thousands, but I also love giving a simple yet profound message to a friend; both are such a privilege. The shape or size ultimately doesn't matter; what does matter is that the prophecy connects people with the heart of their heavenly Father. The simplest prophecy can have the most profound impact if it draws the listener deeply into the heart and intention of the King of Kings.

It's important to understand that prophecy isn't always about the future, despite most secular dictionary definitions. If we see prophecy simply as 'predicting the future' we end up with a very narrow, one-dimensional revelatory experience. The truth is that a lot of the time prophecy involves God speaking into our current reality and circumstances, so that we are better able to understand the here and now through the eyes of God. Prophecy gives us insight into every situation we may face; it enables us to see our past, present and future from God's perspective.

It's also important to clearly distinguish between the authority we place on Scripture and that given to prophecy. We approach them differently. The Bible will always carry greater authority because the very nature of prophecy means that fallible humans are trying to communicate something of the Spirit using limited contemporary vocabulary. We will never get it all 100% right! But as long as we know how prophecy fits alongside scripture, then we can enjoy pursuing this amazing gift, being careful to test everything. Prophecy complements the written Word because it speaks to the *specific* – the specific time, place and people. Both have the power to transform lives and communities.

In the Bible there is a differentiation between Old Testament and New Testament prophecy and we need to ensure our approach to prophetic gifts comes with a New Testament mindset. Under the old covenant the prophets were commissioned by God to speak his words with an absolute divine authority, and the people listening to these words were expected to treat them as the 'very words of God'. There was no room for error and the response to a false prophet was to have him stoned (Deuteronomy 18:20).

But under the new covenant, with the outpouring of the Spirit prophecy becomes a gift that is freely available to all believers. The nature of prophetic ministry has changed: it is no longer just for an isolated group of old-school prophets, but is something we can all partake in. We all have direct access to God and we can all hear his voice. The context of prophecy is now the community of faith and it is embedded in love and fellowship. The church has become the centre of prophetic activity: a family of listeners, who discern God's voice together. We all get to join in, which is wonderful, though of course this means things are going to be messier.

A Gift of the Spirit

Chapters 12, 13 and 14 of Paul's first letter to the Corinthians provide us with many keys to understanding the New Testament take on prophecy. In these chapters we read Paul's theology on spiritual gifts as well as some of his instructions on best practice. And the context for these chapters is of course community – it's the body of Christ working out how to best use the gift so that the whole fellowship is edified.

It's worth pointing out that when Paul writes about the outworking of prophecy in the church, the church communities he had in mind were different from what we might think of as 'church' today. When the Corinthian church came together (1 Corinthians 14:23) it would have been in someone's house, with perhaps up to 50 people present. It certainly wouldn't have been in a designated auditorium, with hundreds present. So when we examine Paul's instructions for worship and prophetic ministry we have to see them through first-century eyes, where the expression of church was through extended households.

Prophecy is a gift from the Holy Spirit, a manifestation of the Spirit's presence, given for the common good (1 Corinthians 12: 7, 10). We don't receive spiritual gifts for our own benefit; rather they are given to us so that we can be channels of God's love and blessing for others. In fact one of the key signs of maturity with the gift of prophecy is the absolute knowledge that **we prophesy for the benefit of others.** It's a gift to be given away. The prophetic picture the Holy Spirit recently gave me to illustrate this truth is of someone standing by a waterfall and collecting the water in pristine buckets, and then quickly giving the full buckets to others for their refreshment: the more the buckets are given away, the more new buckets can be filled.

It should be a great encouragement to us that the Holy Spirit distributes his gifts *just as he determines* (1 Corinthians 12:11); ultimately it's not up to us – we can't manufacture or conjure up a prophecy, rather we anticipate the overwhelming generosity of the One who is always there to reveal truth to us and equip us to bless others.

Paul tells us to eagerly desire spiritual gifts, especially prophecy. We don't have to get worried and perplexed by the concept of spiritual gifts – they are simply ways that we can express God's love to people – tools in our spiritual toolkit. The gift of prophecy is for strengthening, encouragement and comfort, and we are commanded to ask for it, seek it, and use it to build each other up.

Here is a testimony from my friend Joanna's wedding:

> *Shaun and I really value prophecy. Over the years we have been incredibly encouraged through hearing God speak into our lives. We love that when we talk to God, he answers us with love. Therefore, it was really important for us to include the gift of prophecy in our wedding because we wanted to hear what God had to say to us on the most important day of our lives.*
>
> *During the service a few close friends gathered around us to both pray and prophesy over us. One of these was my aunt: in the run-up to the wedding she had been praying for us and God had given her an extended prophecy that she then read out to us. It was a beautiful moment as we heard her relay the words God had given her; we heard what plans God had for our marriage and how much he loved us as a couple and as individuals.*
>
> *We had invited some non-Christians to the wedding, at least three of whom contacted us directly after the day to ask us what the prophecy part was all about. They were really surprised to hear that God speaks back to us when we pray to him! We were really happy to have included prophecy in our wedding, even if a few people may have found it rather odd. We want our marriage to be centred on God, and therefore hearing his specific words to us on our wedding day was the perfect way to acknowledge that*

What is Normal?

In many churches today, even those that are comfortable with spiritual gifts, there can sometimes be an uneasy relationship with prophetic ministry. Often the perception of prophecy is that it is only for certain people: the leaders and the spiritually 'elite'. People regularly stepping out in the gift may be thought of as suspicious or odd. And the so-called 'average' Christian believes that this amazing gift is out of their reach:

"It's just not for me; it's not my thing."

I really want to challenge that mindset. If someone turned up on your doorstep one day and presented you with a huge and beautifully gift-wrapped present, would your response be, *"It's not my thing"*? And yet how many times have we refused to open the door to the Holy Spirit's gifts because we have ruled ourselves out of being valid recipients.

Looking at the teaching of the New Testament it is apparent that the gift of prophecy is available to all:

> *I will pour out my Spirit on all people ... and they will prophesy*
> Acts 2: 17-18

> *Eagerly desire gifts of the Spirit, especially the gift of prophecy*
> 1 Corinthians 14:1

> *For you can all prophesy in turn so that everyone may be instructed and encouraged*
> 1 Corinthians 14:31

Prophecy is not an optional extra for a select few. Rather it's an essential tool, part of the Lord's provision, so we that we can be effective disciples and do his work. We are not all called to be prophets, but we can all prophesy. (We'll look at what it means to be a prophet in the next section of the book). There is a great need in our comfortable, Western churches to rekindle a desire and expectation, indeed a desperation, for the prophetic gifts. They are given for the great good of the church and they are given so that, in the words of John Wimber, everyone gets to play.

I love being in a church culture where prophecy has pretty much become normalised. It's expected, it's accepted; no-one bats an eyelid if someone gives someone else a prophecy. It's become well-embedded in our culture – from big Sunday services to missional communities to friends meeting up to pray for each other; from prophetic art as part of our worship to prophetic appointments for business leaders in our church family.

And that's how it should be. Prophecy shouldn't be seen as something just for leaders, just for the 'super-spiritual', or just for the 'wild and wacky' people. It's something that all God's children can use – and can become really good at using. Prophecy should be normal.

This is my friend Elaine's story:

> For many years I viewed prophecy as being rare and very serious, partly because I was attending churches where it was seldom exercised and there was a lack of expectation. Before sharing what I believed God was saying to me, I felt I needed to be pretty certain I had got it right, and that it would be well received. I would never share anything that didn't make sense to me except with close and understanding friends.
>
> But recently, as I've learnt much more about the gift, I now know that prophecy is not rare because we have a super-generous, communicating God who wants to talk to us. Yes, there is a serious element to prophecy, but it always brings life, freedom, joy and often laughter. I do not have to work it all out or answer the question 'Why?'
>
> Rather, I can safely leave it to others to weigh, accept or reject prophetic words or pictures, as I share them with a bit less fervour and a lot more gentleness.

For me, prophecy has become a joy to pursue rather than a burden to be shouldered.

Why Do We Need Prophecy in Our Churches?

Fundamentally the church needs prophecy because it brings the 'now' word of God – speaking into our specific contexts. The Bible is essential for general guidance, but for the church to be all that God wants it to be we've got to be able to hear the 'now' word, so we are being led by the Voice, not just the written words. The church was born through the Spirit, and the call on every Christian community is to keep in step with the Spirit; a strong prophetic culture plays a key part in developing a sensitivity to the Holy Spirit's leading.

There are many benefits to having prophecy alive and active in our churches – here is a brief overview of the key ones:

• Prophecy resources discipleship

As we saw in Chapter 1, being able to hear God's voice for ourselves is vital for every disciple of Jesus. But the gift of prophecy is also a great tool for any disciple-making culture, with the potential to deepen and sharpen the process to a significant degree. Discipleship happens when people are both drawn deeper into covenantal relationship with God **and** equipped to do the works of his kingdom.

Prophecy resources discipleship by first of all speaking to people about their true identity in God. When I'm prophesying over people I love to ask God questions about how he sees them, how he has perfectly created them, and then speaking out words which really affirm them in who they are. Prophecy reveals the affections of God's heart towards us and gives us greater levels of security as we hear his words of affirmation. As Paul states in 1 Corinthians 14:3, prophecy strengthens, encourages and comforts us.

But true prophecy does more than draw us deeper into the love and affirmation of our heavenly Father; it also releases us into our God-shaped future, empowering us to step out in faith and change the world. Prophecy reveals how the Lord has called, equipped and gifted each one of us for ministry. I think about some of the really significant prophecies spoken over my life and how they keep me moving forward; they motivate me to keep pressing in to take hold of everything that Jesus has for me.

Mature prophecy bears good fruit in the lives of disciples: greater passion for Jesus and closer alignment with his words and ways; faith renewed and built up; fullness of life in the Spirit; hope restored.

- ## Prophecy empowers mission

Prophecy is of tremendous benefit to the church because as we learn to hear and communicate God's will and intention, his Spirit will always be directing us out into the world. As our spiritual hearing becomes clearer and sharper we will inevitably find ourselves tuning in to the missional heartbeat of God.

A mature perspective on prophetic ministry sees prophecy as a gift not just to be kept within the confines of the church, but one to be taken outside the church walls, and to be used as an effective tool in evangelism. Yes, you can prophesy over non-Christians! In fact, as long as you are sensitive and skilled in your approach and language, you find many people who don't yet follow Jesus are really receptive to hearing a word of hope and encouragement from the Lord.

The prophetic also has a key role to play in informing our missional strategy as the Spirit reveals to us where the harvest fields are. We need eyes to see where the harvest is ready, and a prophetic church is one where we are regularly asking the Lord of the harvest to show us which are the key communities, networks and people groups to focus our mission on. Whom has the Holy Spirit been preparing to receive the message of the kingdom?

A natural outworking of the prophetic being so ingrained in the culture of our church here in Sheffield is that when people start a new missional community, one of the first things they will do is **seek God together** for a missional vision.

My friend Danny is someone who is both a passionate evangelist and gifted prophet, and I love to hear his stories from the 'front line' where these two ministries often collide with glorious results.

Two of us were preparing to go into town and share the gospel with people. [Danny does this on a very regular basis]. We spent an hour praying before we went out, and during this time of prayer God gave me two prophetic pictures. One was of a Chinese man; the other was of a woman with polka dots on her raincoat. God told me that I would meet these two people that day.

As we left I felt the Holy Spirit tell me that he wanted us to walk into town rather than getting the tram, as we usually do. As we began walking I spotted the same Chinese man that God had revealed to me earlier. He was pacing backwards and forwards, looking very worried.

I went up to him and told him that God had asked me to speak to him.

He told me that he was very concerned because his wife was pregnant and the hospital had told them there was something wrong with the baby. We prayed for him on the street and God told me to tell him to go straight home and pray with his wife. He ran off, and that was the last I saw of him, but before he went he told me, "If Jesus helps my family then I will dedicate my whole family to him." God's words to me were, "You've done your bit, now let him go and do his bit."

We walked into town and had an amazing time, leading many people to Jesus and sharing prophetic words with lots of people, but all day I kept thinking about the woman in the polka dot raincoat. Just before we finished I spotted her. I ran up to her and said something like, "We're not mad; we're from a local church and are here today praying for people." It turned out she was a Christian who was going through a really tough time. We were able to really encourage her, and she was incredibly moved that God had sent us to meet her that day.

These two encounters did much to build my faith: God knew exactly who we were going to meet that day. He's teaching me to listen carefully to him and then step out in obedience.

Another time I was in town when it was really crowded. I was in the middle of all these people when God highlighted one woman to me. It was like everyone else was out of focus, but she was sharply in focus. I knew God wanted me to speak to her. I got into a conversation with her and she told me of her many worries, especially concerning her daughter. At that point God gave me a simple prophetic picture and word to share with her: a picture of God sprinkling gold dust all over her, and the words that she was incredibly precious. As I shared this her face lit up. She was overwhelmed by God's love and made the decision to give her life to Jesus. She then told me to stay there while she went to get her daughter. They came running back together and I got to pray with them both and led her daughter to Jesus as well.

- Prophecy provides vision and direction

If we have ears to hear, and hearts submitted, God will always speak into his church and show us where to go. A God-given, Holy Spirit inspired vision is vital for every church: it informs every decision and gives us a common purpose. As the Bible tells us, without vision the people perish (Proverbs 29:18).

A mature prophetic culture, that carefully stewards revelatory gifts, will help provide a sense of godly purpose and direction. The Good Shepherd will lead his flock. I love being in a church where the leaders regularly set time aside to seek the voice of God for wisdom and direction, and where prophetic people are actively encouraged to speak into the decision-making processes.

- Prophecy speaks against social injustice

A church with a strong prophetic culture will be one that is in tune with God's heart for the poor and oppressed, and will not be content with acquiescing to the injustices of the society around it. God's intention for his church is that it is a prophetic servant community, representing his heart to those who need him most.

A prophetic church has a role to play as a spokesperson of God's righteousness and justice. When we open our spiritual eyes and see the world around us from the perspective of God's kingdom, the Spirit will be ready and willing to speak to us about how we can get our hands dirty and act prophetically on behalf of those who need a touch from the King.

• Prophecy fuels prayer

There is a very close connection between prophecy and prayer, and a listening culture in our churches will do much to catalyse a praying culture. When we come together to pray we want to be praying from a perspective of, *"Your kingdom come, your will be done,"* and spending time **listening first** allows us to catch a vision for how God's kingdom is breaking out in the particular context and what God's will is.

The most exciting method of prayer is finding out what God wants to do, and then asking him to do it – in this respect the Holy Spirit is leading our prayers and they are aligned with the thoughts and intentions of God. And if we are praying according to God's leading, we will have much more faith for answered prayers.

In our church in Sheffield we have done much to ensure that the prophetic ministry and intercessory ministry are working closely together: we want the intercessors to know what the prophets are seeing and hearing so that they can pray for the prophecies to be fulfilled. We've also recognised that prayer meetings need to have lots of space for listening and for prophetic gifts to be encouraged.

Recognising (and teaching people about) the many benefits of prophecy will do much to allay the fears and misconceptions that can arise when we set out to grow a prophetic culture in our church communities. I hope you can see how prophecy shouldn't be perceived as just an add-on or optional extra for a particular group of people to enjoy if they want to. An attitude of, *"We can take it or leave it,"* is robbing the church of the opportunity to get its hands on a remarkable gift. As we shape the culture of our churches, small groups and missional communities, let's be encouraging each other to *eagerly pursue* prophecy (1 Corinthians 14:1) and give plenty of opportunities to practice on each other.

Simple Steps to Hearing God for Others

I'm going to finish this chapter by getting to the 'nitty-gritty' of how we can all start using the gift of prophecy.

There are many different approaches to engaging with prophecy [and in *The Prophecy Course*[3] there are step-by-step instructions for a number of suitable exercises to develop confidence in using the gift] but here I want to suggest three simple approaches.

At the end of the last chapter I set out a structured approach to tuning in to God's voice, and of course we can use exactly the same process to get ourselves in a place where we are ready and available to hear his voice for others; these suggestions take us on from that place:

1. Use the Lord's Prayer to engage in listening prayer for others

Take each phrase from the Lord's Prayer and use it as a prompt for asking God questions – and listening for the answers – as you seek to prophesy over someone. For example:

> **Our Father** : How do you want this person
> **in heaven** to know the assurance of your
> Fatherhood today?

> **Your kingdom** : What will it look like for your kingdom
> **come, your** to be made manifest in this person's
> **will be done** life today?

> **Give us today our** : What particular provision are you pouring
> **daily bread** out on this person today?

....

[3] Cath Livesey – *The Prophecy Course 2nd Edition* (Accessible Prophecy, 2013)

Forgive us our debts, as we also have forgiven our debtors	: What are your words of grace to this person today?
Lead us not into temptation	: What is the path of righteousness you have laid out for this person to walk today?
Deliver us from the evil one	: How can I pray your protection over this person today?

2. Use your sanctified imagination

God gave us our imaginations as a source of blessing, and as long as we offer them back to him he delights to use them as a means of revealing his heart and thoughts to us. One of my favourite ways of prophesying over people is to imagine that Jesus is standing in front of the person and then look to see what Jesus is doing – with eager anticipation. I often see him give the person a particular gift, or lay his hands on them to bless them, and it's such a joy to then communicate this to the person.

3. Honing a prophecy over time

Most prophetic ministry in our churches today takes the form of spontaneous prophecy, where we speak out what we sense God is saying pretty much there and then. But there is another approach to prophecy, which is when we craft a prophecy over a period of time, by writing it down and then repeatedly coming back to it, honing it and refining it with the Spirit's guidance. This approach doesn't fit so well in today's society where we want instant results all the time, but it's a discipline well worth cultivating, and it may well have been the methodology employed by some of the Old Testament prophets.

A few years ago at a special service of inaugurating our new senior leaders, I was asked to speak a prophecy over our church. I spent six weeks working on this prophecy, regularly praying about it, writing and rewriting it, and submitting it to others for inspection. By the time

I delivered it in front of many hundreds of people I was confident that the words I were speaking were completely aligned with God's heart and it was a real joy to journey with him as he unpacked the message for me.

Part Two

Prophets

Chapter 4

The Ministry of Jesus

In this section of the book I want to turn our attention to New Testament 'prophets' – a word used to describe a certain type of person with a particular God-given role. Reading the New Testament, particularly Paul's writings and the book of Acts, generally leads us to the conclusion that whereas we can all use the **gift** of prophecy, some people will have a particular calling to prophetic **ministry**; a defined role as 'prophet'.

For example, we can compare 1 Corinthians 14:1 with Acts 15:32:

> *Eagerly desire gifts of the spirit, especially the gift of prophecy.*

> *Judas and Silas, who themselves were prophets, said much to encourage and strengthen the believers.*

The gift of prophecy is available to all, and a prophetic church is one in which everyone is confident in hearing God's voice. However, some people have a particular ministry of being a prophet. To keep with our sheep metaphor, there are some sheep in Jesus' flock that have particularly good hearing, and have a special grace from God to help other sheep hear more clearly.

I'm convinced that in order for any church to develop a healthy and holistic prophetic culture, two of the most important questions it needs to ask are:

- Who are our prophets?
- Are they equipping us to hear God?

In order to do this we need to move away from an Old Testament view of what a prophet is, and grasp the new covenant paradigm. We also need to see that prophets are alive and well today. Their ministry is not one that died out centuries ago, but is one that the 21st century church would do well to both understand and embrace.

In order to fully understand what a New Testament prophet is we are going to use a particular framework, an approach to thinking about ministry and calling that is rooted in Paul's theology of the church, and has significant implications for discipleship.

One of the teachings that has been most empowering for us as a church in Sheffield has been teaching on the *five-fold ministry*, based on Ephesians chapter four. As we've dug into the text and explored all that Paul intended when he wrote this particular letter, we have seen so much fruit as *all* members of the church have been equipped to participate in the work of the kingdom. And it's been the catalyst for releasing a lay leadership determined to walk into all that God has for them.

This teaching challenges the way we think about church, leadership and ministry. It challenges the hierarchical assumption that only some people are 'called to ministry', leaving the laity as passive *receivers* of ministry. Instead it puts leadership and ministry into the hands of every disciple. The five-fold ministry of Jesus is represented in his whole body, not just in an elite few.

Fundamentally this is about identity, and embracing the fact that each and every one of us are a gift to the church and have a key role to play in ensuring that it reaches unity and maturity. Understanding how God has designed and shaped each one of us means that we don't have to strive to be someone or something different. We simply enjoy the grace that comes with knowing what he's called us to do.

Unity, Diversity and Maturity

Ephesians is not a typical letter of Paul's in that rather than being written to one specific church and addressing a particular set of problems, it is thought to have been intended as a 'round-robin' letter for churches throughout Asia Minor, with generic content. It's a letter to **the** church, rather than *a* church; a letter to the church **about** the church. In many ways it is Paul's best thinking on church and how it should operate.

In verses 1-16 of Ephesians 4 Paul sets out how the church of Jesus is designed to function, starting with unity, then going on to diversity, and finishing with maturity. Paul's heartfelt plea for every disciple is that they should *live a life worthy of the calling you have received*; and his main concern for the church, the body of Christ, is that it should represent the life of Jesus. Paul then sets out how we can achieve these two goals: by maintaining unity, embracing diversity, and equipping each other to reach maturity.

In verses 7-13 Paul writes about how diversity is expressed within the unified body and lays out what the roles of all believers are to be within the church:

> *But to each one of us grace has been given as Christ apportioned it ... So Christ himself gave the apostles, the prophets, the evangelists, the pastors and teachers, to equip his people for works of service, so that the body of Christ may be built up until we all reach unity in the faith and in the knowledge of the Son of God and become mature, attaining to the whole measure of the fullness of Christ.*

What a wonderful picture Paul presents to us of a mature church: working in perfect unity, and perfectly representing everything Jesus is. This is a picture of God's people embodying the very fullness of Christ.

And we get there by taking hold of the special gift that Jesus generously gives each one of us. As The Message translation puts it:

> *That doesn't mean you should all look and act the same. Out of the generosity of Christ, each of us is given his own gift.*

What Paul is saying in this passage is that Christ has given the church particular portions of grace in the form of five ministries, and that these are distributed throughout the whole body. Every Christian has been given grace from Jesus to fulfil one of five roles; *each one of us* has a calling to be one of five types of people: apostle, prophet, evangelist, pastor or teacher. The Greek word used in verse 7 is *hekasto* which literally means 'to each and every person'. The five-fold ministries are for **everyone**, not just leaders. And Jesus has given them to us so that the church can be all that Jesus has called it to be, fully representing him in the world. The church needs all five.

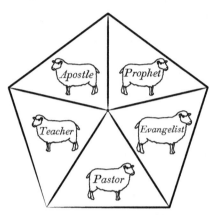

The beautiful thing about the five-fold ministries is that together they represent the ministry of Jesus. Each one reflects a key element of the ministry of Jesus, and their diversity expresses the diversity of ministry seen in the life of Jesus. In fact Jesus is the fullest representation and demonstration of all five roles: Jesus is the perfect apostle, prophet, evangelist, teacher and pastor. A remarkable synergy happens when all five are working together in harmony and unity of purpose within a community because that is when we get a truly Jesus-shaped church.

The only way the church can function as intended, is if every believer is serving in the role and ministry Jesus has created them to do. That way we all contribute to the building up of the church to maturity. It is only when all five gifts are fully released to equip the body that we will be able to truly reflect the full measure of Christ and express his glory to the world around us.

In the words of Alan Hirsch, *"Jesus has given the church everything it needs to get the job done."*[4]

....

[4] Alan Hirsch & Tim Catchim - *The Permanent Revolution* (John Wiley & Sons, 2012)

We've all had grace apportioned to us; we have all been built with a purpose. God does not expect you to be who you are not – but he does want you to be all that he has made you to be. He has made each one of us to fit a certain place where we can serve him best, where he can shower us with grace. Our calling is to be different – but to be one.

Gifts vs Ministry

At this point I want to tackle two questions that often arise when we start to talk about the diversity found in the body of Christ:

- What do we mean when we use the words 'gift' and 'ministry' - how are we to best understand and utilise these words?
- How are we to make sense of the places in his New Testament letters where Paul presents us with varying lists of spiritual gifts and ministries?

Starting with the first question, in some ways it can be beneficial to use the word 'gift' as an umbrella term to encompass everything that God has given the church to equip it, whatever form it takes. As we read Paul's letters, and those particular passages that speak of gifts for the church, it would seem that from Paul's perspective, there are two broad categories of 'gift':

- Gifts that come in the form of people e.g. an evangelist
- Special abilities given to an individual e.g. the gift of healing

Both types can be described as a 'gift'. However, for the sake of clarity (and being pragmatic) I think it is helpful to distinguish between a **ministry** and a **spiritual gift**, particularly in relation to the prophetic. The five-fold ministry roles in Ephesians 4 are about identity, about **who we are** – the way Christ has made us as he gives us as a gift to his church. We pick up this strong sense of vocation in the first verse of Ephesians 4. The key word is the Greek word *klēsis*, which we translate as 'calling':

> As a prisoner for the Lord, then, I urge you to live a life worthy of the calling you have received.

Paul then goes on to use nouns to describe the five ministries in verse 11:

> So Christ himself gave the apostles, the prophets, the evangelists, the pastors and teachers.

This is a list of ministries that we are called to embody, not activities which we engage in. The call from God is to be one of five types of people. The gifts of Jesus to his church are **actual people**.

Spiritual gifts, on the other hand, are not vocations or permanent roles; rather they are brilliant tools in our spiritual tool kit. The gifts listed in 1 Corinthians 12:1-11 are gifts of the Holy Spirit. The key word is *manifestation* in verse 7 – these gifts are manifestations of the presence of the Holy Spirit. As I've said in Chapter 3, the gift of prophecy, like all spiritual gifts, is available for everyone. So regardless of what your five-fold ministry is, the gift of prophecy is available to you – and what a great gift it is!

So going back to our first question:

- Ministries are gifts of Christ in the form of people.
- Spiritual gifts are special abilities given by the Holy Spirit.

When we come to compare 1 Corinthians 12:7-11, 1 Corinthians 12:27-31, Romans 12:4-8, and Ephesians 4:7-13, in each of these passages we see Paul's favourite metaphor for the church: the body of Christ. But we see different items on the lists – how are we to make sense of this? Context is key. It's also important not to get distracted from the big picture that Paul is communicating: we all need each other.

- The context of 1 Corinthians is a church that was facing some serious issues: divisions, jealousy, immorality, misuse of spiritual gifts in corporate worship, and abuse of the Lord's Supper. The message of the church being one body, with many mutually dependent parts, was vital for a church infected by pride and individualism. The reason for the list of gifts and ministries at the end of chapter 12 is to give examples to the Corinthians of how they all had a vital part to play in the body of Christ.
- Romans was written to a church struggling with a growing rivalry between Jews and Gentiles, and as a result was unable

to function as a united body. Paul's emphasis in chapter 12 is on sacrificial living: he calls the Roman Christians to stop arguing and start serving each other in love. And, as Paul goes on to explain with some particular examples, a great way they could do this is by using the special abilities God had graciously given each one of them.

- Corinthians and Romans are written to specific situations with specific problems and the lists they contain are not exhaustive; rather they are examples to make a point. The Ephesians passage is written to the church in general and is more of a blueprint. The purpose of the gifts listed in Ephesians is to bring the church to the full measure of Christ. We can therefore conclude that the most comprehensive list is probably the Ephesians one.

- When we compare the different lists we see that sometimes Paul is writing about ministries and sometimes he is writing about spiritual gifts. As we've already seen, in Ephesians 4 the gifts are actual people (ministries), whereas the gifts in Romans 12 are special abilities (spiritual gifts).

- Paul seems happy to have a mixture of people-gifts (i.e. ministries) and special abilities (i.e. spiritual gifts) in his lists; this is evident from 1 Corinthians 12:27-31.

Paul's central message in each of these passages, and one that we really need to take hold of, is that God has not designed the church with a few people who are so multi-talented that the rest of us are redundant; rather, we all need each other.

Now you are the body of Christ, and each one of you is a part of it.
1 Corinthians 12:27

The Five-Fold Ministries

From him the whole body, joined and held together by every supporting ligament, grows and builds itself up in love, as each part does its work.
Ephesians 4:16

One of the joys of discipleship is discovering with Jesus the particular way he has designed each one of us so that we can fully play our part in the work of the kingdom. How has God wired you?

Jesus has put varying degrees of ministry and leadership into the hands of every disciple: we are all empowered and equipped for service. The dynamic is one of grace: as it says in verse 7, *to each one of us grace has been given as Christ apportioned it.* We've all been given a measure of grace to fulfil our particular ministry role. We're all in the game together.

So it's really important to start to recognise and unpack the role we've each been given. The best way to do this is to spend some time examining the five different ministries and work out which one best reflects the way God has made you.

One word of caution: with the five ministries the emphasis is on role and function, rather than position or title, and this is an important distinction to make. Calling oneself a 'prophet' does not carry any assumption of special anointing or leadership, and it doesn't equate to having a mature prophetic ministry – it simply means that Jesus has shaped you with that particular role to play.

Here is a brief overview of each of the five roles, giving a generalised definition and description – the aim is to highlight the key distinctive marks and 'flavour' of each ministry so that we can better understand the special contribution each one brings to the body of Christ. The explanation of each ministry is largely derived from the pattern we see in the Bible, but there is also the evidence we have gathered over time as we've dug into and explored each of these five people-gifts of Christ with many different people.

So what follows are very much broad brushstrokes. It's not about putting anyone in a box, because every believer has been created by God as a unique individual with his or her own special contribution to make. Rather it's about looking at the big picture of how Jesus has designed his church and seeing how we all fit somewhere in this picture. Each of the five roles brings a unique perspective and sensibility to the mix. Together they provide the church of Jesus with everything it needs to be built up to maturity.

• Apostle

The Greek word for apostle is *apostolos*, which means 'sent one' and, along with prophet, is at the pioneering end of the spectrum of ministries. Apostles like to be on the move, and more than any other ministry they give the church forward momentum. They initiate change and innovation; in fact the way to spot them in any organisation is to look for the people who are forever starting up new projects.

The word 'missionary' derives from the Latin translation of *apostolos* and central to the role of apostle is the sense of someone who has been sent on a mission from God. They are people who love to plant new initiatives and pioneer breakthrough. A great New Testament example of an apostle is of course Paul, who is the very embodiment of a 'sent one,' and whose ministry was based around missionary journeys and planting churches.

Apostles are people of vision: they enjoy dreaming of 'big picture' possibilities and then making them happen. What to everyone else may look like a dead-end, to an apostle would be an opportunity to knock a wall down and move the whole church through the gap. Apostles are hard-wired to discern open doors on the mission field:

> *Though I am free and belong to no one, I have made myself a slave to everyone, to win as many as possible.... I have become all things to all people so that by all possible means I might save some.*
> 1 Corinthians 9:19-22

> *But I will stay on at Ephesus until Pentecost, because a great door for effective work has opened to me, and there are many who oppose me.*
> 1 Corinthians 16:8-9

The apostolic role is foundational for the church (Ephesians 2:20) and this is reflected in the fact that it comes first in the list of ministries in Ephesians 4. Apostles are not more important than the other roles, but they are the ones who lay the foundations for new initiatives – they will pioneer in places where no one else has been before. And not only are they expert pioneers, but they are gifted at growth and multiplication, able to mobilize and empower groups of people for maximum kingdom advancement.

We can clearly see the apostolic ministry in the life of Jesus because he was the ultimate 'Sent One': sent into this world by his heavenly Father to rescue us from our sin and give us new life and purpose. He went from town to town, always on the move, and in the midst of this ministry he trained up his small group of apprentices so they could multiply his work and take it to the ends of the earth.

• Prophet

This is a brief description because in the next chapter we will explore the nature and function of the prophetic role in much greater depth.

Prophets are particularly attuned to discern God's voice and equip others to hear him. Revelation comes easily to them, and their role in the body of Christ is to communicate what they sense God is saying in any situation.

The prophetic ministry is marked by a passion for God's heart, a hunger for his presence, and a concern to call the people of God to greater covenantal faithfulness and obedience.

As we look at the New Testament we see a number individuals who embodied the role of prophet. Agabus was a member of the early church who had a recognised prophetic ministry (Acts 11:28 and 21:10); and Philip's daughters were all known as prophets (Acts 21:9).

Jesus is our perfect and complete prophet; in fact he is the definitive revelation of God. He is the one who most perfectly shows us what God is like. During his ministry he spoke prophetically of the future (Matthew 24 and 25) and discerned the hearts and minds of people (Matthew 12:25, Luke 9:47). His prophetic words to a Samaritan woman led to a town being transformed (John 4). He was prophetic in his actions (Matthew 21:12 and 19) and prophesied his own future (Matthew 17:12). He also fulfilled hundreds of Old Testament prophetic words.

• Evangelist

The role of the evangelist is to bring the good news, in fact the Greek word for evangelist – *euangelistes* – means one who brings and tells the good news. Their ministry is defined by a willingness and passion to share the Good News of Jesus with as many people as possible. They effectively spread the gospel message and inspire others to do the same.

Evangelists love to seek out and spend time with non-Christians – in fact they often prefer to spend their time out in the wider community rather than being with fellow believers in church. They have a natural boldness about sharing their faith and are skilled at making the gospel relevant to people outside God's kingdom.

Evangelists are enthusiastic people gatherers and storytellers. They are natural networkers, good at connecting with people, usually with sociable and engaging personalities. They tend to be effective and persuasive communicators. They enjoy discussion and sharing their point of view. They find it easy to draw others into discussion about Jesus.

They are passionate about Jesus and passionate about people. They help to ensure the church is outwards focused. They are focused on the mission of God – the message of God's love. They draw our attention to the broken world around us.

When we read the book of Acts we can see Philip operating in the ministry of an evangelist: he was a highly effective preacher of the gospel, who helped plant the church in Samaria.

> *Philip went down to a city in Samaria and proclaimed the Messiah there. When the crowds heard Philip and saw the signs he did, they all paid close attention to what he said ... They believed Philip as he proclaimed the good news of the kingdom of God and the name of Jesus Christ, they were baptized, both men and women.*
> Acts 8:5-6,12

There is no better example of an evangelist than Jesus. He is the Good News: every aspect of his life, ministry and nature is the best news we could possibly have. As we read the gospels we see the incredible compassion Jesus had for the least, the last and the lost. He was also committed to training up his disciples in evangelism, empowering them to heal the sick and preach the good news (Luke 9).

• Pastor

The role of a pastor is to shepherd God's people, bringing much needed care and protection. Their focus is on the church community, desiring it to be a unified and loving family; often acting as the 'glue' that holds the community together.

Along with evangelists, they have a real passion for people, and are highly relational. Like a shepherd, they keep a protective eye over the flock, and are quick to spot anyone in trouble or needing help. They can easily empathize with others and love to bring encouragement and comfort.

Words that describe a pastor are: compassionate, gracious, merciful, hospitable, patient, good listener.

Pastors are motivated to see all God's people mature to their full potential and will sacrificially devote time and energy to an individual's growth and development, carefully nurturing them, and being prepared to bring godly challenge where necessary. They are also good team builders, creating environments were everyone in a group can flourish and feel valued.

Barnabas was someone in the early church who demonstrated a pastoral heart. In Acts 15:36-41 we read about Barnabas' compassion and mercy for Mark, demonstrated in the fact that he was prepared to give him a second chance. In fact the name 'Barnabas' means 'Son of Encouragement' (Acts 4:36).

Jesus is the perfect expression of a pastor. He calls himself the Good Shepherd who is prepared to lay down his life for the sheep. Throughout the gospels we see that he was moved by compassion for the people around him, for example in Mark 6:34:

> *When Jesus landed and saw a large crowd, he had compassion on them, because they were like sheep without a shepherd.*

- Teacher

Fundamentally the role of a teacher is to help the church understand biblical truth, so that disciples can grow in comprehension and wisdom. It is about helping people have God's perspective on their lives and the world around them, through theological insight. They bring an incredible strength and stability to the body of Christ. The teacher's motivation is that disciples gain deeper and fuller understanding of the truth contained in the Bible, and that they are then able to apply it to their lives.

Teachers are hungry to learn. They enjoy research and the gathering of information. They love to read and study the Bible, and then explain what they have learnt in ways that make it easy for people to grasp. They are energized by the opportunity to pass on truth that they have taken hold of themselves. They have the ability to make the complicated simple and memorable.

We find a good New Testament example of a teacher in Apollos:

> *He was a learned man, with a thorough knowledge of the Scriptures. He had been instructed in the way of the Lord, and he spoke with great fervour and taught about Jesus accurately… He vigorously refuted his Jewish opponents in public debate, proving from the Scriptures that Jesus was the Messiah*
> Acts 18:24-28

Jesus of course is the ultimate teacher. He is *the* Truth. He has the words of eternal life (John 6:68). Near the start of his ministry he sat down on a hillside and taught the crowds that had gathered around him a message that was so profound, challenging and simple that the people were stunned:

> *When Jesus had finished saying these things, the crowds were amazed at his teaching, because he taught as one who had authority, and not as their teachers of the law.*
> Matthew 7:28-29

So that's our overview of the five ministries that Jesus has given his church in the form of people-gifts. They are all equally vital and important. If any one is missing the church is substantially less equipped to fulfil its calling. God wants us to celebrate the diversity he has placed among us; in fact it's the very diversity contained within the five-fold that enables the church to attain *unity in the faith*.

Maturity for every disciple comes through not only embracing our own ministry role, but also allowing ourselves to be refined and shaped by the other four. Because every role is an expression of Jesus, every one of us should be seeking to attain a level of maturity across all five ministries.

We're not all called to be pastors, but we are all called to care about people and the pastors teach us to care. We're not all called to be evangelists but we are all called to be witnesses and the evangelists teach us to witness. We're not all called to be prophets but we are all called to listen to God, and the prophets teach us how to hear the voice of our Good Shepherd.

And with each role comes both freedom and responsibility: the freedom to be exactly who God has made you to be; the responsibility to become a **mature expression** of that ministry so that all may be blessed and equipped. If God has made me to be a prophet I can enjoy all the incredible blessings that come with that role, but at the same time I have a responsibility to shape and refine my prophetic ministry so it reflects Jesus and equips his church. It's vital that we remember that each of the five ministries is at heart about **equipping others**. The main calling of a prophet is to equip all disciples to hear God's voice.

You are probably reading this book because you are interested in prophecy and how to hear God better. It's really important that prophets understand and appreciate the other four ministries. It's important that in a book on prophecy we pause a while to consider the vital work of the other four. A mature prophetic ministry will be marked by a desire for the whole five-fold to prosper.

Chapter 5

The Role of Prophets

In the previous chapter we've seen how God has designed us all with a special role to play and a unique contribution we can make as we get to grips with Paul's teaching on the five-fold ministries.

In this chapter we're going to look in depth at the role of the prophet and the unique shape of this particular people-gift of Jesus. If you happen to be a prophet I hope what follows will help you understand the incredible blessing you are to the body of Jesus; and if you are not a prophet I hope this will lead you to better appreciate this particular ministry.

'Prophet' is certainly an interesting (and challenging) title to give to anyone. It conjures up images of outsiders. The socially inept. The mentally unbalanced. The wild-eyed, long-bearded purveyor of judgement. And, yes, I do know a few of them like that.

Would you want to be labelled a 'prophet'?

But of course Ephesians 4 teaches us that a prophet is simply one of five people-gifts that Jesus has given to the church. There is nothing particularly special or unusual about being a prophet. All five ministries are vital. Each is an expression of Jesus' own ministry. In fact the purest expression of the prophetic ministry is when it is working in beautiful harmony and humility alongside the other four, each part committed to seeing the others prosper and mature.

And when I stop and think of the prophets I know, what I see is a rich and beautiful kaleidoscope of Jesus-followers, with differing personalities and expressions of the ministry; friends and associates among whom are my heroes. People who have sacrificed so much for the sake of the kingdom and who simply want to serve their Lord with the gifting he has given them. Most of them are also very down-to-earth and 'normal'.

Understanding Prophets

In order to grow a healthy and mature prophetic culture in our churches we need to understand prophets, so that:

- we can identify them, disciple them, equip and release them
- they can function at their full potential
- they can be an amazing blessing to the church

As I said in the previous chapter, in giving the church the five ministry gifts Jesus has provided us with everything we need in order to 'get the job done'. But if the church is turning a blind eye to the role and function of the prophet, a key part of Jesus' great design for his church is going to be missing.

The truth is that prophets have a weighty contribution to make to the body of Christ, but, of the five-fold, the prophet is usually the one that is least understood. Misconceptions about prophets and prophecy abound! And because of this lack of understanding prophets have a sad history of being a nuisance rather than a blessing. Human nature tends to fear the things it doesn't understand and in my experience there are two types of repeated negative patterns stemming from misunderstanding:

- **Cycle of rejection, brokenness and criticism:** misunderstanding leads to the prophet being, and feeling, rejected; out of this brokenness the prophet becomes critical and judgemental of the church, which in turn leads to more rejection.
- **Cycle of control and rebellion:** misunderstanding results in the church heavily controlling the prophet, whose response becomes rebellion. The more the prophet rebels, the more the church tries to control him or her.

Both types of negative cycle lead to the prophet becoming withdrawn and isolated. Rather than being part of the church community, and ministering as one who has a soft heart towards his or her fellow believers, the prophet ends up being a critical voice outside the church – manifesting the spirit of independence and refusing to submit to any counsel or correction.

Speaking as a prophet myself I heartily urge all you prophets out there to do all you can to break these destructive cycles through love, grace and humility. There is too much at stake to walk in step with rejection and rebellion. And I would encourage everyone reading this book to make a determined effort to really understand prophets, and in doing so to normalise and de-mystify the prophetic ministry.

One of the great benefits of the intentional embrace of the five-fold ministry here in our church has been the validation and normalisation of the ministry of a prophet. Looking at prophets from the perspective of Ephesians 4 has done much to ensure they are better understood. It has allowed prophets to fully participate in the ministry of Jesus, ensuring that they are not sidelined in preference for the more easily understood ministries. And the five-fold mindset has enabled the prophetic ministry to mature, as it learns to appreciate and be shaped by the other ministries.

The Unique Contribution Prophets Bring to the Body of Christ

I want to now spend some time looking at the many different contributions prophets bring to the work of Jesus in the church and world.

1. Listen and perceive

Prophets are particularly attuned to hear and communicate the heart of God. Of course everyone can learn to hear God's voice, but with prophets revelation usually comes easily and naturally – sharper and clearer. Using Paul's analogy of a body (Romans 12:5, 1 Corinthians 12:12-31, Ephesians 4:12) prophets ensure that the church has eyes to see and ears to hear. When the rest of the church has perhaps acquiesced to a dullness of hearing, prophets are there to keep a clear channel of communication open.

They see clearly with sharp, future-focused eyes. They look ahead, look further, and can perceive the future picture, the 'what could be' of kingdom potential.

They see what is on the horizon, acting as 'watchmen'. The biblical picture of a watchman is that of someone stationed on the walls of a city in order to see the approach of an enemy (1Samuel 14:16, 2 Samuel 13:34 and 18:24). The same word is also applied to prophets in the Old Testament (Jeremiah 6:17, Ezekiel 3:17, Isaiah 62:6). The word for watchmen in the Hebrew is from the root *tsaphah*, which means to lean forward, to peer into the distance, to observe and to wait. Part of the role of a prophet is to protectively stand watch over the church, keenly looking out for any threat from the enemy, discerning light from darkness, truth from lies.

Because of their keen spiritual sight prophets have a role to play in releasing vision – they see the bigger picture of where God is calling us and enable us to lift our eyes up and perceive future potential. They speak hope and purpose to the body of Christ, inspiring and encouraging forward momentum. They also help people understand the here and now through the eyes of God. They speak out a heavenly perspective on our current reality, helping us understand the times and seasons.

2. Equip

A key part of the calling and responsibility of any prophet is to help people hear God for themselves, so that every one of Jesus' sheep can discern his voice and obey his leading. A question I regularly ask of prophets I'm mentoring is, *"Who are you passing this on to?"*

This can be quite a challenge because there is often something in the prophetic personality that prefers to go it alone. They are quite content to be left alone to seek God. There is a real cost for many prophets to open up their private spirituality to others and become accessible. A sign of maturity in a prophet is a heart to train other people and being prepared to draw people close to them so that imitation can happen. The principle of multiplying our lives into others is one that all prophets need to embrace. There are so many opportunities to come alongside other people and teach the basic principles of hearing God and allowing imitation to take place.

A question that all prophets need to ask themselves is: *"Am I dying to self so that I can invest in others and equip them to hear God?"*

3. Orientate

Prophets have a deep hunger for God, a passion for his presence, and a desire for everyone to draw closer to Jesus. Their passion for God's heart means they are always re-focussing attention back on God, seeking his perspective on any situation. Their role in the church is one of orientation, constantly turning people back to Jesus, drawing us back to hear the heartbeat of God. They encourage people towards a closer relationship with God, provoking encounter with his manifest presence.

The prophets of the Old Testament called people to live faithfully in covenant relationship with God. And a key part of the role of New Testament prophets is to keep calling the people of God back to faithfulness and obedience, awakening a passion in people for the greater things of God. They are the voice in our midst that reminds us to prioritise both seeking and obeying what the Lord is saying to us.

Prophets naturally tend to focus on the spiritual dimension of life, being uninterested in the more pragmatic and mechanistic aspects of church. Their desire is always to live out of the revelation of God's heart and truth with as much integrity as possible.

A mature prophet will have a graceful and godly influence on those around them, causing hearts to seek God's call and agenda, even if it is personally costly.

4. Prepare the way for Jesus

John the Baptist was the last – and greatest – of the old covenant prophets (Luke 7:28), but when we examine his ministry we find few prophetic utterances recorded in the pages of scripture. His significance was not in the quality or quantity of the prophecies he delivered; he was the greatest prophet for the simple reason that he prepared the way for the Messiah and bore witness to him.

> And you, my child, will be called a prophet of the Most High; for you will go on before the Lord to prepare the way for him.
> Luke 1:76

Our understanding of John's role and ministry informs our perspective on new covenant prophets. There is something about the mature prophetic ministry which opens up the way for Jesus, that goes ahead of the Lord and makes hearts and minds ready to receive his message.

Prophets are often forerunners. They can facilitate that necessary moment of kingdom breakthrough – not by strategic implementation, but through prophetic declaration and action – so that our earthly context comes into alignment with the kingdom of heaven. They have a role to play as catalysts; stirring up the church into action so that the message of Jesus will have maximum impact. They are often happy to go ahead of the crowd, ploughing up the ground, and being instruments of breakthrough.

5. See creative solutions

Prophets often have the ability to stand back from the immediate and see creative solutions and develop a vision for situations others don't see. They are often highly intuitive and can think outside the box. In this way a prophet is a valuable part of any team.

Many of the prophets I know are creative people, and the prophetic ministry and creativity often go alongside each other. Both are fundamentally about expression, and the arts provide a means of expressing God's message in creative and arresting ways. A prophetic church will be one with a multi-faceted and creative expression of prophecy.

6. Intercede

Prophets love the chance to get alone with God and wait on him – to seek his face – and out of that place flows prayer and intercession. Prophets are often people who have a strong intercessory call on their lives, which is why we often find them in our church prayer meetings. Their natural tendency to focus on God's heart means they can become real champions of prayer in the church, encouraging others to make prayer and intercession a priority.

Prophets are especially sensitive to the battle going on in the spiritual realm, discerning the work of the enemy, and motivated to engage in spiritual warfare. They are wired to see beyond the physical and recognise where spiritual strongholds need tearing down.

Living in Tension

I hope you can see how much value prophets can bring to the body of Christ. But I also want to acknowledge some of the challenges and tensions of being a prophet. It's not always an easy calling and there is the potential to be overwhelmed by frustration if our hearts are not set on the bigger picture of building the church up to maturity.

To be a prophet is to be someone who has a passion for the heart of God, and that means feeling God's heart for the world. It means being prepared to reach out and connect with the very emotions of Almighty God. It's both an immense privilege but terrible burden to feel God's pain, longing and anger. I'm always incredibly moved when I read the book of Jeremiah and see how that particular prophet had to carry the heartbreak of the God whose people had turned their backs on him.

There is also the very real challenge of living in the 'gap' – prophets have an especially keen awareness of the tension between the 'now' and the 'not yet'; the 'actual' and the 'ideal'. They are simultaneously focussed on the glory, nature and values of God and, at the same time, sensitive to the existing reality in the world around them, with all its injustice and unfaithfulness.

Because of this the prophet is someone who at heart desires to challenge the status quo, bringing an alternative consciousness to the existing order of things. They question everything that does not seem to honour God and draw us closer to him, question everything that does not reflect the values of God's kingdom. If this questioning is done in the context of good relationships and commitment to community then it is a gift that prophets bring to God's people, one that edifies, empowers and sharpens. But when such questioning takes place without mutual love and honour it simply feels like criticism, and the prophet becomes an unwanted irritant.

Because of their primary concern for God and his values and his vision for the world, prophets tend to sense situations where his values are not reflected. They tend to be very strong on truth and righteousness and are prepared to speak against oppression and injustice. They will confront ungodly contentment with the existing order of things, calling and provoking for change. They call the people of God to live differently, to be counter-cultural and to choose God's ways over the ways of the world.

There is often a tendency in prophets to see everything in black or white: it's either of God or it's not, it's either holy or unholy. They struggle with shades of grey, which causes tension when everyone else is reasonably happy with a bit of greyness. Anything that might compromise their integrity is going to cause heartache for a prophet.

Finally, their sensitivity to, and focus on, the spiritual realm can lead to tension with other members of the church who have a more pragmatic and seemingly less 'spiritual' approach. Prophets find it hard to appreciate and value strategy and decisions that are not birthed out of clear revelation: why would you want to make any move unless you have a clear and unambiguous mandate from the Lord?

In order to navigate this life of tension prophets need to guard their hearts carefully. They have to learn to take their frustrations to Jesus and not grow weary of seeing the gap. They have to beware judgement and critique of others. And they have to regularly engage with the discipline of thanksgiving and maintaining good relationship with their church community. At the end of the day it's a tremendous privilege to have the call as a prophet, to see further and to be taken into God's confidence.

The Council of the Lord

In the pages of the Old Testament we can find a perspective on the prophetic calling that reminds us of the solemn and holy nature of this call.

In Jeremiah 23 there is a long passage (verses 9-40) in which false prophets are denounced. It doesn't make particularly cheerful reading. But false prophets were a recognised problem in the time of Jeremiah.

You may be familiar with the story in 1 Kings 22 in which the king of Israel and the king of Judah are planning on going to war together against Ramoth Gilead. So they gather 400 prophets together and ask them whether or not they have the Lord's blessing. And their answer is, *"Yes, go to war – God will give you victory".*

But the king of Judah doesn't quite trust these four hundred prophets and asks for a second opinion. So along comes Micaiah the one true prophet – whom the king of Israel hates, for *"he never prophesies anything good about me"* – and to cut a long story short Micaiah prophesies the king of Israel's death in the coming battle. And lo and behold, that's what happens. The armies of Israel and Judah are defeated and the king is dead.

So on the one hand you have 400 false prophets telling the king what he wants to hear, and on the other hand the one true prophet who resists that temptation and tells the king exactly what he *doesn't* want to hear – and who subsequently gets thrown into prison.

As far as I know Jeremiah 23 isn't directly addressing this story, but it is clearly speaking about the problem of false prophets. And in the midst of a withering denouncement of these people we find verse 18:

> But which of them has stood in the council of the Lord to see or to hear his word? Who has listened and heard his word?

I've always been fascinated by this verse. It raises hope in me that there is a place that true prophets are invited into, a holy and intimate place: the council of the Lord.

The Hebrew word translated 'council' is *sôd* (pronounced *sode*). The Strong's Concordance[5] definition is:

> *A session, that is, company of persons (in close deliberation); by implication intimacy, consultation, a secret: - assembly, counsel, inward, secret (counsel)*

It occurs about twenty times in the Old Testament and is translated differently depending on context, but it always has connotations of intimacy among a group of people. It can be used to describe a group of people who conspire together, sharing their secrets and plans; or can be used to describe the relationship of a group of people in sweet fellowship, who share and are intimate together.

- an intimate circle of friends
- a secret council
- a sacred assembly

The same word is used in Psalm 25:14:

> *The Lord confides in those who fear him.*

and Amos 3:7:

> *Surely the Sovereign Lord does nothing without revealing his plan to his servants the prophets.*

So according to Jeremiah 23:18 a true prophet is someone who is taken into God's confidence; someone who has access to the Lord's circle of friends; someone who is permitted to stand in the sacred assembly. And as prophetic people we should have confidence that we have an invitation to this place.

As I've been meditating on this passage recently it has really struck me that the council of the Lord is a place where we have to ruthlessly lay down our own agendas; we cannot take our own agendas into that holy place, we leave them at the door. Part of the journey of growing in prophetic ministry is learning the discipline of laying down all our own agendas. In many ways this is the definition of humility. True prophets are only interested in God's agenda.

[5] James Strong - *Strong's Exhaustive Concordance of the Bible* (Abingdon Press, 1890)

Prophets are Disciples First

It's vital to recognise that prophets are first and foremost disciples. So our primary focus is not our ministry but the simple yet hard daily choice to follow Jesus. We need to adopt a posture where, if God took away our prophetic ministry tomorrow, we would still be fine because all that matters is loving and obeying the King.

So for a mature prophetic culture to thrive in our churches, leaders need to be intentionally discipling prophets, and prophets need to be whole-heartedly embracing this – choosing to submit their lives to those who hold them accountable; receiving support, challenge and encouragement.

And prophets need to be leading a **balanced life**, mirroring the three-dimensional life of Jesus. When we pay close attention to the model that Jesus left us we see that he lived out his life in three perfectly balanced relationships: **Up** with his heavenly Father, **In** with his friends and followers, **Out** with the broken, hurting world around him. This simple and biblical framework will enable us to thrive, not just survive, as prophets. It will ensure that both our life and ministry are balanced, mature and fruitful.

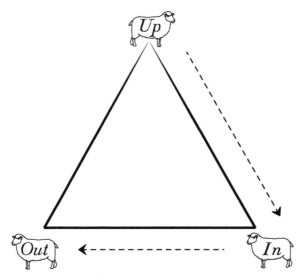

We were created to be three-dimensional beings, and if one dimension is weak or missing, our ministry will be out of balance. To flourish as a disciple **and** a prophet we have to pay attention to areas that do not come naturally to us and intentionally work on them. We have to make a commitment and effort to have all three dimensions in balance.

UP

To mature and thrive as a disciple *and* prophet we first of all need to ensure that we have a strong and growing relationship with our heavenly Father. We need to be intentionally pursuing friendship with God and regularly engaging with spiritual disciplines. Just because we can hear God's voice easily does not negate the need to be reading and meditating on the Bible. On the contrary, the more time we spend soaking our minds and hearts in the written Word, the greater the depth and substance of our ministry.

A healthy upwards relationship with God is more than praying for a few minutes every morning; it's about taking the presence of God with us wherever we go. Jesus told his disciples that he could do nothing by himself, only what he had seen the Father do (John 5:19). He could observe the Father at work because he walked so closely with him. God invites us to that same level of intimacy.

Here are some questions we can ask ourselves as we pursue a strong UP dimension:

- Do I have a regular discipline of prayer and Bible reading?
- Am I a passionate worshipper?
- Am I hearing God's voice in the Bible?
- Am I regularly encountering the presence of God?

IN

It's vital that prophetic people have a strong inward dimension to their lives, fully embedded in community, with healthy relationships with other believers. God created us to be social beings and his design for his church is that we are one body. In fact the love that Christians have for one another is the mark that identifies us as Jesus' disciples (John 13:35). We are all called to live out our faith alongside others.

It is unfortunate, then, that there is always a danger for a prophet to become isolated and unaccountable. Isolation is a temptation for prophets. They can hear God so well by themselves it's easy for them to end up thinking, *"I don't need anyone else – I can hear God!"*

But commitment to community is part of the deal for New Testament prophets. In order to have a balanced and fruitful ministry we have to overcome the challenges of community and pursue deep fellowship with our fellow believers.

Here are some questions to ask ourselves as we seek to grow a healthy IN dimension:

- Am I committed to my church community?
- How are my relationships with my Christian friends?
- Am I accountable about my life and my prophetic ministry?
- How easy is it for me to trust people?

OUT

To be truly balanced and holistic, prophets also need a strong engagement with the world around them and a missional heart. For many prophetic people this is their weakest dimension: reaching out to non-believers doesn't come naturally to many prophets. To express their faith with people who don't yet know Jesus is very much stepping out of their comfort zone.

But to be a happy and thriving disciple and prophet, we have to have a strong outwards dimension to our lives. Jesus said he would make us fishers of men and that means even the most introverted prophet has a call to leave the comfort and safety of their prayer closet and get out into the world.

I think it's good to think outside the box in terms of how prophets can engage with OUT in ways that feel natural and true to who they are. It doesn't have to involve awkward and out-dated methods of evangelism. Prophets love seeking God's heart for people and a natural extension of that is to seek God's heart for the world around them. Working in partnership with the Holy Spirit to see the people he has been preparing to receive the gospel can be such a fruitful and liberating way to reach out to people. And tuning in to God's heart for social justice can give prophets the propulsion they need to truly engage with the world around them.

Here are some questions to ask ourselves as we intentionally grow our outward dimension:

- Do I have a compassion for the lost?
- Do I leave time for relationships with non-Christians?
- Can I see what the Holy Spirit is doing in my local community?
- Am I representing God's heart and nature with my words and actions?

Elje's Story

I want to finish this chapter by sharing with you the story of my Dutch friend Elje, who has recently been on a journey of discovering that she is a prophet:

> As a young girl I was in a church that you could probably describe with the words of 1 Samuel 3:1, "In those days the word of the Lord was rare; there were not many visions". Maybe there were in other churches, but not in the place I grew up. So as I tried to talk about the visions I saw and the words I heard God speak, no one recognised what was happening to me. And just like Eli advised the young boy Samuel to lay down and get back to sleep, I was told to ignore it and stop thinking about it.
>
> The reactions of the people around me didn't prevent the Lord from speaking to me, but sadly it took me many years before I understood it was God's voice that I was hearing – that these were his words and he was speaking out loud in his world.
>
> The real breakthrough for me came in studying Ephesians 4 and understanding that some people are called by God to be prophets. I took the five-fold ministry test[6], and realised that the things I enjoyed doing, like being quiet in the presence

---

[6] You can find out more about the Five-Fold Ministries and take the test at www.fivefoldsurvey.com

of God, or seeing his ways in nature or in small things, were a valid expression of the person God has created me to be and of the ministry he was calling me to.

There were few living examples of prophets around me, and only rare glimpses of the gift of prophecy being exercised, so it was necessary to fully trust my Father in this. Maybe he had made me a prophet, but I wasn't at all sure what a prophet exactly is or does. An image of Elijah came to mind … but that wasn't me, was it? So who am I? And what is God asking me to do or to be?

I discovered that it's as simple as spending time with him: connecting to him, focusing on him and being open for his still small voice, sometimes not more than a quiet whisper. These all give me an insight in the heart of the Father. And I guess that's the place a prophet is called to be, that's what a prophet is called to do. That's what I am called to do.

In a way a lot of the experiences I had in the past made sense now, once I had this lens to view them through. I wasn't 'gifted' or 'weird' or even a 'new-age-kid'. My heavenly Father was just showing me things and helping me to understand things when there was no one around to help me out. As a prophet God has given me insight into situations, into the lives of other people. He shares his wisdom with his beloved children to comfort them, to strengthen them and maybe just because he loves to do this.

Over time I feel that God is healing me from the rejection, the ignorance and the misunderstanding of the past. He has brought me something new. He has given me a firm foundation, a massive rock, to place my feet on, instead of the swamp of incomprehension and fear. And from this firm and steady rock I feel secure to listen to my Father for others, to share the words or pictures he gives me in prayer. And it's brilliant to serve others in expressing the way he made me to be, doing the things I'm called to do.

Chapter 6

A Pathway to Maturity

If you're reading this book as someone in any kind of leadership capacity I hope by now that you can see how much a contribution prophets can potentially make to the body of Christ. But I know that for many of us the prospect of actually leading and releasing prophets can seem quite daunting. Our response is still:

"Help! I've got a wacky prophet in my church!"

The theory is fine; it's the reality of having to make it work that brings challenge to the average church. We need to find answers to these questions:

- What is the pathway that allows prophets to develop and mature and become all that they have been created to be?

- How can we ensure they are also being effectively discipled and held accountable?

- How do prophets fit in a culture of discipleship and mission?

- How do prophets multiply themselves and their ministry?

I've spent many years working with prophets: I've taught them, trained them, discipled them, encouraged them and disciplined them. Plenty of mistakes have been made along the way, but I really believe that it is possible to create a win-win culture – where leader, prophet and congregation are all happy: prophet-friendly churches.

A Culture that Enables Prophets to Thrive

Let's just pause a moment and consider the word 'culture'. You've probably noticed I use it quite a lot. To be strategic it's important to address issues of culture before structure. And whenever we talk about creating culture, we've got to start with language. You may have heard the saying that 'language creates culture' – and in our experience it's true – what we say, how we say it, and the mediums we use to say it will create a certain culture.

The issue is that many of us are leading communities of people and creating a culture accidentally because we haven't intentionally thought through the language we use to shape that culture.

We need to approach culture making with serious intentionality, allowing a shared language and vocabulary to create the culture God is calling us to shape.

So as we start to look at how we can shape the culture in our churches, so that it becomes one that prophets can really thrive in, it's important to consider the language we will be using.

We can set the culture in our churches in such a way that it becomes a really healthy environment for prophets to be 'grown in' and flourish – imagine a nice greenhouse! Intentionally using words like 'discipleship' and 'accountability' will do much to shape a successful culture.

1. Discipleship

Prophets are first and foremost disciples. Prophets need to be engaging in discipleship just like everyone else. Discipleship is about our whole lives and to be whole as a prophet we have to be whole as disciples.

We saw in Chapter 1 how discipleship is at the very heart of our Christian faith. It's about choosing to follow in Jesus' footsteps, hearing him and obeying him. It's much more than just becoming biblically literate and following spiritual disciplines. It's about growing into the character and competency of Jesus.

As Dallas Willard puts it:

"Discipleship is the process of becoming who Jesus would be if he were you."[7]

As we seek to grow a culture of discipleship that prophetic people can engage with it's very important that we don't confuse the ability to hear God clearly with spiritual maturity. It's all too easy to look at an anointed prophet who is getting accurate revelation and therefore assume that he or she is a mature disciple of Jesus. Anointing is not an indication of character. Putting the emphasis on discipleship above gifting helps the people of God to embrace wholeness and maturity. It also helps to avoid any kind of spiritual hierarchy.

Discipleship doesn't happen in isolation; rather it's choosing to be led by others. As we engage with the process of discipleship we make the decision to both follow others and to disciple others. Discipleship has to be done the right way – holding it out in such a way so both leader and prophet feel they can engage with it.

A culture of discipleship should be life-giving to a prophet. Their passion for God's heart, their natural tendency towards radicalism and faithfulness, their ongoing desire for greater spirituality, should all translate into wholeheartedly embracing the discipleship process. Who wouldn't want to become more like Jesus? Prophets are usually desperate for investment, longing for people they trust speaking into their lives.

But sadly there are many prophets who are not engaging in discipleship; they are choosing not to submit to and be led by other people. Why? I think it all comes down to questions of perception and mutual trust. Most prophets will run a mile from anything they perceive as control. They will also be deeply suspicious of godless structures or anything that does not appear to be 'Spirit-led'. And trust is a huge deal for the majority of prophets: *"Who can I trust with these revelations? Who can I trust that they won't try and control me?"*

Of course there is all the difference in the world between control and accountability, we just need to be incredibly careful with the language

[7] Dallas Willard - http://www.dwillard.org/articles/artview.asp?artID=71

we use, so that one is not confused for the other. Control is telling people what to do and how to do it; a culture of high control offers no freedom for disciples to explore the call of God for themselves. In complete contrast a culture of high accountability lets people see and own their own vision – the role of the leader is then simply to hold people accountable to what God is asking them to do.

Accountability won't always come naturally to a prophet, but a culture that actively promotes and places a high value on it will gently encourage the prophet to see it as something positive which will enable them to become more like Jesus.

It's worth noting that some leaders are reluctant to actively disciple people who are more prophetically gifted than them. The insecure leader is going to ask, *"How can I lead this highly anointed prophet who hears God better than I do?"* But this is not fully understanding the process of discipleship. Discipling others is not about hearing better; it's about holding people accountable to what God is saying to them. It's about calling people to fruitfulness and engagement with God's kingdom. It's about allowing others to imitate us as we pursue relationship with Jesus.

As we seek to grow a culture of discipleship, where prophets do not fear control, and where leaders are confident in leading those more prophetically gifted than them, careful and intentional use of language is key:

I think you're great; I'm committed to invest in you; I want to help you follow Jesus more closely and grow into all he has for you. I'm not going to tell you what to do, but I'm going to hold you accountable for hearing and obeying whatever God is saying to you as we discern it together.

What we also need is a good methodology, which is where our next point comes in.

2. Invitation and challenge

Jesus was a truly remarkable leader. He took twelve very ordinary men, spent three years training and investing in them, and at the end of that period of time he had done such a great job of discipling them that they went on to change the world. And when we look carefully at the gospel accounts we see that the key methodology Jesus used with them was that of continually calibrating invitation and challenge. He created a culture that was highly invitational, where he regularly affirmed his disciples and welcomed them into deeper relationship with him. But he was also incredibly challenging with them, speaking directly against ungodly behaviours and mindsets, and calling them to the challenge and discipline of being representatives of the kingdom of God. It was certainly not a cosy and easy ride for those twelve men, but Jesus knew exactly what he was doing with them in creating a highly inviting but also highly challenging culture for his disciples to grow within.

We too have to learn how to balance invitation and challenge as we lead and disciple people. To work with and raise up prophetic people well requires a culture of both invitation to relationship and challenge to change. Too much challenge and not enough invitation will quickly lead to prophets backing off and becoming really discouraged and alienated. But a highly invitational and encouraging environment, that lacks robust challenge, will result in a lazy and passive prophetic culture.

Creating a culture that successfully calibrates invitation and challenge enables the prophet to grow effectively as a disciple first, and then also in ministry. Prophets need leaders who will speak wisely into every aspect of their lives as Jesus-followers, as well as help them to refine their gifting. Thinking in terms of **character** and **competency** can be helpful here:

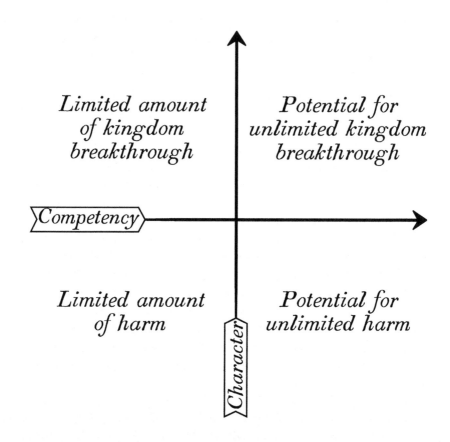

We want to raise prophets who are growing into both the character of Jesus and the competency of a mature prophetic ministry:

- the **character of Jesus**: lives marked by faithfulness, obedience, and the fruit of the Spirit
- the **competency of Jesus**: growth in giftedness, skill, aptitude, multiplication

Investment that carefully calibrates invitation and challenge will enable every prophet to grow in both character and competency.

Again, let us consider the kind of language that creates this culture of invitation and challenge:

I'm inviting you to deeper relationship with me, and I give you access to my life. Because I'm committed to you, and see the huge potential in you, I will bring healthy challenge to you when necessary, so that you can grow in character and competency as both a disciple and as a prophet.

3. Community

New covenant prophets need community. It was all very well for the likes of Jeremiah and Co to minister in isolation, but under the new covenant the church has become the centre of prophetic activity, and a commitment to community is the deal for everyone, regardless of what our five-fold ministry is. Jesus never let his disciples do anything by themselves: they even had to find a donkey as a pair.

So a strong culture of community, enhanced by the right sort of language, is going to be key for the healthy development of prophets.

We value you, we're committed to you, come and be part of our community and let us help you become all that God has got for you.

As we saw in the previous chapter, there is a tendency for prophets to become isolated. The most dangerous place for prophetic ministry in a church is right on the edge of things – a long way from the leadership, a long way from the central heartbeat of the church, a long way from accountable relationships. So we have to create an environment that draws prophets close to the centre and ensures that they are firmly embedded in community; a place where prophets feel loved, accepted, valued, and invited in. We want to create a culture that communicates that the prophets and all that they bring are valued.

Prophets need a sense of belonging, so that when they bring a word to the church, they are listened to because they are part of the family. A leader's job is to help prophets find a supportive community. But more important than that is the need to create a culture where prophets can gain a vision for community, so that they are able to maintain a soft heart towards the body: a heart to build up the church.

A strong community will naturally create trust, and it's worth recognising that many prophetic people have to overcome their fear of judgement and rejection in order to mature and thrive. It's really important that prophets feel that they can trust their community not to reject them if they share revelation.

And a strong community will create an environment of healthy submission and mutual respect: the prophet is happy to submit to his/her leader because they are part of the same family.

4. Strong culture of service

One of the things we have deliberately sought to develop here in my church in Sheffield is a strong culture of service around the prophetic.

As we've done this we've found that this creates a healthy environment in which prophets can develop. Hearts and minds have changed as people have come to realise that spiritual gifts are beautiful opportunities to serve other people. As it says in 1 Peter 4:10:

> *Each of you should use whatever gift you have received to serve others, as faithful stewards of God's grace in its various forms.*

Our attitude should be: *"How can I use my prophetic gift to serve other people and the purposes of God in them?"* And as we develop this mindset the focus shifts from ourselves – me and my gift – to others and how we can best serve them.

We can shape the culture by frequently re-stating what it is we're about:

We're here to serve and bless people.

In fact nearly every time I gather a group of people together to do prophetic ministry I will say this. And when I gather people to be on the many prophetic teams I lead, having a servant heart is what I look for probably above anything else. It's worth considering who are the people who are willing to use their prophetic gift in the hidden ways; I'm always so encouraged by those who will gladly go away and seek God for a prophetic word for a 'name' I have given them because it reveals a true heart to serve others.

Leading Prophets

Having looked at issues of culture, let's now turn our attention to how church leaders can get the best out of prophets. The absolute key is good relationships: there is no substitute for this. If we're going to lead prophetic people well we have to invest in and build relational capital with them.

- Prophets love vision, so take time to carefully communicate your vision for the church/community/city with them, and invite them to support you as you work to see the vision realised.

- Understand them and validate them as individuals, as disciples, and as prophets. This is where an appreciation of the whole five-fold ministry is so helpful. Have one or two prophets that are close enough to you as a leader so that you understand their world and their language. Include prophets who are part of your support system as a leader – those you trust and of good character – who are regularly praying for you and listening to God on your behalf.

- Be really clear about expectations: what am I as a church leader expecting of you as a prophet? What are you expecting of me as a church leader?

- Offer them your ear: let them know that you will listen to them – that you want to hear what they have to say.

- Give them permission to spend lots of time with God. This sounds really simple, but it's amazing how the busyness of church life can actually take people away from time with God. It's never a waste of time for a prophet to spend time with God – it's the basis from which everything flows. So as we lead them we need to give them lots of permission to do this. In fact from time to time we need to release them from other obligations so that they can devote time to this.

- As a leader be secure enough to receive the questioning of a prophet, as long as it comes from relationship and right dialogue. Hear the heart of the prophet. Take what is said and weigh it well.

- Give them opportunity with boundaries. Prophets need an outlet – it's important that they have lots of opportunities to exercise their prophetic gift – but you as a leader can set the constraints of that outlet. Empower them with clear boundaries.

- Finally, as a leader, to value and honour prophecy you have to do it yourself; so be prepared to talk about what God is saying to you, and be a good role model for prophetic ministry.

It's worth saying that at the end of the day not everyone will follow you; there will always be at least one prophet who refuses to engage with discipleship, community and submission to leadership. With people like that it's a mistake to stop them prophesying altogether; you just have to put very tight parameters around them so that they can't do any harm. So, for example, tell them that all prophecies they receive have to go directly to you. That way, they have some outlet.

Potential pitfalls

As we develop a culture where prophetic people can be a real blessing to the church we need to be very real about the particular temptations that prophets may face. Our aim is always for a mature expression of prophetic ministry, and if both leaders and prophets are aware of these potential pitfalls, discipleship and maturity will be benefitted.

- **Spiritual pride and self-righteousness**

  There is a temptation to think that just because God is using you to deliver some amazing prophecies you must be better than everyone one else, that God likes you more than other people, and that you are by far the most spiritual person around. Unfortunately this can also be exaggerated by other people's assumptions that prophets are 'special'. Some prophetic people actually go around with a manufactured glow of super-spirituality and if anyone questions their actions or words then accusations of quenching the Holy Spirit start to fly. This, of course, is very dangerous.

- **Seeking to impress others through prophecy**

  We are all vulnerable to the desire to please and impress people, and there is a temptation to prophesy what we think people want to hear. This is particularly the case in a public setting, for example if we have been asked to give words to people at the front of church. If people know you are prophetic then there can often be pressure and expectation to prophesy a 'wow' word over someone, and it's very easy to find ourselves succumbing to people-pleasing. To overcome this temptation we have to be ruthlessly obedient to the Holy Spirit and lay down all our agendas.

- **Refusing to let words be weighed by others**

  The Bible clearly tells us to weigh prophecy carefully, and we should all be willing to have our prophecies weighed by other people. None of us are infallible; but for some of us the temptation is to take on the attitude of, *"If my prophetic words are rejected, you are rejecting me as well."* Getting things wrong, and having our words rejected, is actually a vital part of the journey to maturity for any prophet – it hurts, but it's really good for you!

- **Independence**

  The temptation that many immature prophetic people face is the desire to do things their own way; to follow their own vision. This tends to manifest itself in a lack of submission to leadership or failure to embrace the common vision of the church. Some prophets are so focused on their own way of doing things that they become unteachable, refusing to accept correction or any kind of feedback. This is all rooted in pride.

- **Assuming a false responsibility for ensuring prophecies are responded to**

  If God gives you a prophetic word for the church, it is your responsibility to deliver it to the church leaders. It is not your responsibility to ensure they respond. If the leaders don't appear to be doing anything about it, you simply have to have peace that you did what God called you to do. The prophet is simply the humble messenger.

- **Abuse, control and manipulation**

  I think that there is sometimes a danger of vulnerable people becoming over-dependent on a prophetic person, especially if the prophet is encouraging them to keep coming back to them to get a word for their lives. And this is the sort of scenario that can end up leading to control and manipulation. There is a danger of using prophecy to gain influence and control over people's lives which we need to be very wary of.

The best way to minimise these pitfalls is a culture of discipleship and accountability, where the emphasis is on love, humility and servant-heartedness, and where leaders have strong relationships with prophetic people.

Apostles and Prophets

I want to finish this chapter by looking at the one relationship that has the potential for incredible kingdom breakthrough if we get it right, but much heartache and frustration if we get it wrong: the relationship between apostles and prophets.

We can see from both Paul's letter to the Ephesians (2:20) and the life of the early church that the two ministries are closely associated, and are indeed foundational for the church. Both ministries are pioneering and like to question the status quo. Both are concerned with vision and change. Any missional movement needs the remarkable synergy that happens when the two come together, but natural tendencies inherent in both ministries can easily push them apart.

I happen to be a prophet who is married to an apostle, and so I have first hand experience of both the strengths and weaknesses of this partnership of ministries! We look at things very differently. Apostles are focused on kingdom strategy, innovation and growth, looking to get the greatest number of people empowered and equipped. Prophets are focused on God's heart and values – doing something the **right** way is more important than getting a result. Prophets tend to see apostles as being too pragmatic and mechanistic; apostles are inclined to view prophets as being ineffective dreamers who never achieve any significant results.

But even though we approach things differently we really need each other. Apostles need prophets to provide the discernment to know which of the 101 great ideas is actually God's idea and to ensure that it's carried out via godly values; prophets need apostles to bring the **application** of the prophetic – to sharpen and refine the vision so that it can become reality. An apostolic culture without the prophetic can easily become almost business-like, focused too much on effective systems and methodology. A prophetic culture without the apostolic will be passive and have little impetus for multiplication.

When we consider the missional call on the church we can see that we will have greatest impact when the two ministries are working together in harmony and understanding. Their roles are different but equally important. Missional breakthrough is initiated by the prophet seeing and discerning: the prophet helps the people to hear where God is calling them to, identifying the good soil to receive the message of Jesus. The apostle then provides the strategy and reproducible systems and forward momentum so that God's mission can be carried out with the maximum effectiveness.

My personal testimony is that I've seen the greatest levels of fruitfulness and growth in my life and ministry when I've been directly led by an apostle. Yes, it's tough at times, but prophets need apostles.

Part Three

Revelation

Chapter 7

The Spirit of Truth and Revelation

What is revelation? It's a word that is used frequently in prophetic circles, but what does it actually mean? And what does the word 'revelation' actually tell us about God? As we spend some time digging into its meaning we will come to see that revelation is inherent to the very nature of God. Not only is the dynamic of revelation central to the concept of the Trinity, but revelation is at the heart of the gospel.

What does the word 'revelation' mean? Dictionaries define it along these lines:

> *Unveiling; disclosure; uncovering; exposure; when something is made known that was previously secret or hidden.*

When we have a revelation about something, we see it for what it really is. We 'get it'; we understand the deep truth about it. Revelation is all about:

- making known the hidden truth
- unveiling reality
- helping blind eyes to see

As we turn our attention to the subject of revelation, we are first of all going to focus on the Person who brings revelation to us.

I can't write a book on prophecy and not have at least one chapter on the Holy Spirit. In fact I've come to see that the two subjects are inherently related and inseparable: you can't have one without the other. The One is the personification of the other.

We prophesy **through** the Holy Spirit.

The Holy Spirit is **the One who reveals**.

In fact the Holy Spirit is the answer to the cry of our hearts that says, *"Father, I want to be more prophetic!"* The Father's answer is always, *"I have given you the Holy Spirit"*.

So at this stage in the book it's right that we start to examine who the Holy Spirit is and the work he does in the lives of disciples. In fact I'd like to tell you about a close Friend of mine who frequently amazes me with his faithfulness and generosity, who is utterly trustworthy and who will lead you on the wildest of adventures.

Let's start with the name Jesus gives this Friend in John chapters 14, 15 and 16: *parakletos*. It's one of those Greek words that has many different translations into English:

Friend
Helper
Comforter
Counsellor
Advocate

I love every one of those words. I love the different nuances and flavours that the word *parakletos* brings with it. Someone who's there to help us with every aspect of life; who brings his comfort to the weary and sad; who counsels us as we face decisions and questions; who would even stand by our side and plead our case in a court of law. In fact an accurate translation of *parakletos* is 'one who is summoned or called to your side'.

Jesus tells us that this *Parakletos* is the Spirit of Truth, and that he will teach us all things and guide us into all truth. In fact Jesus tells his disciples, whose hearts must have been breaking at the prospect of his imminent departure from them, that it is better that he goes away because then the Holy Spirit can be sent to them. Better than Jesus? Better than living 24/7 with the Son of God? This *Parakletos* must be some friend!

And Jesus promises that this Friend will be with us forever. There's not a single day when *Parakletos* is not by our side, ready to help us with anything we need, ready to answer any question we've got.

But the problem is that many of us forget he's there. And when we do remember we treat him more like a switch or tap than Almighty God.

I really think that many in the Western church have been done a great disservice by either a lack of teaching on the Holy Spirit, or by a church culture that treats the third person of the Trinity as a utility. So we turn to him when we need some power, some heat, or refreshment. *"Come, Holy Spirit!"* we pray when we want the spiritual temperature to rise dramatically in our meetings. And then conveniently ignore him the rest of the time.

But he's a person. And he offers us a treasure of infinite worth: friendship.

Friendship with the Spirit is something I have pursued over the last few years and it has radically affected my spirituality. It's actually quite hard to write about because it feels so personal, sacred, and, yes, beyond words. But what I have come to realise is that the Holy Spirit is the **very essence** of love, joy and peace: he constantly ministers these to me - the flow is ceaseless. The only problem is that I am not always paying attention to his work in my life. A good day is a day in which I welcome his presence and stay attuned to him and his fascinating ministry; a bad day is a day when I ignore him or forget he's there.

If we get to know him as a person and pursue friendship with him, then a natural overflow will be seeing as he sees, hearing what he hears and thinking his thoughts. He is the Spirit of Truth and the closer we get to him the more he will lead us into all truth, and the more we will have a heavenly and kingdom perspective. Truth is simply having God's perspective on any situation, and that's the Holy Spirit's gift to us.

The Holy Spirit and Prophecy

For years I've been fascinated by how the Bible portrays the close relationship between prophecy and the Holy Spirit. Prophecy is often the key sign of the outpouring of the Spirit upon people in the Bible. In fact as we read through scripture we see a repeating pattern – the Holy Spirit is released on people and prophecy happens. For example, Numbers 11 records how, as Moses gathered together the seventy elders, the Spirit rested upon them and they prophesied. Two of the elders had remained outside the camp, *Yet the Spirit rested on them, and they prophesied.* When a young man ran to Moses and complained about this, Moses' response shows how much he longed for the Holy Spirit to make all God's people prophetic:

> *"I wish that all the Lord's people were prophets and that the Lord would put his Spirit on them!"*

We see this same pattern in 1 Samuel 10: when Samuel anointed Saul as king he told him that he would have a life-changing encounter with a group of prophets near Gibeah:

> *"The Spirit of the Lord will come powerfully upon you, and you will prophesy with them; and you will be changed into a different person."*

And this is exactly what happened: the Spirit came upon Saul and he started prophesying. A New Testament example is in Acts 19:6:

> *When Paul placed his hands on them, the Holy Spirit came on them, and they spoke in tongues and prophesied.*

So why is there this close link between prophecy and the Holy Spirit? Why is this particular gift so closely connected to the Spirit of God? In John 16:13-15 Jesus describes the ministry of the Spirit in this way:

> *"But when he, the Spirit of truth, comes, he will guide you into all the truth. He will not speak on his own; he will speak only what he hears, and he will tell you what is yet to come. He will glorify me because it is from me that he will receive what he will make known to you. All that belongs to the Father is mine. That is why I said the Spirit will receive from me what he will make known to you."*

The Holy Spirit is the one who gives us revelation of truth. He speaks what he hears; he's the messenger, the channel of revelation. He makes the things of God known to us. And of course that's what the prophetic is all about. This is echoed in 1 Corinthians 2:9-11:

> However, as it is written: "No eye has seen, no ear has heard, no mind has conceived what God has prepared for those who love him," but God has revealed it to us by his Spirit.

> The Spirit searches all things, even the deep things of God. For who among men knows the thoughts of a man except the man's spirit within him? In the same way no one knows the thoughts of God except the Spirit of God.

The Holy Spirit is so closely linked to prophecy because he is the 'Revealer' – he reveals God's heart and mind to us. A fundamental part of his ministry is to search out the deep, hidden things of God and bring us revelation. He is the connection between us and the very heart of the Father. He speaks directly to our spirits and in this way reveals things to us that our natural eyes or ears could never sense. He is the Spirit of Truth who is committed to lead us into all truth and testify to us about Jesus. He is also the 'Gift-giver' – we've already seen in 1 Corinthians how prophecy is a gift from the Holy Spirit, given for the common good. He is the one who loves to generously bestow his gifts on God's children.

A Pentecost Mindset

The most significant connection in the Bible between the Holy Spirit and prophecy is foretold by the prophet Joel and fulfilled at the moment the church was born:

> "In the last days, God says, I will pour out my Spirit on all people. Your sons and daughters will prophesy, your young men will see visions, your old men will dream dreams. Even on my servants, both men and women, I will pour out my Spirit in those days, and they will prophesy."
> Acts 2:17-18

At Pentecost the Lord poured out his Spirit on the waiting followers of Jesus, and everything changed. The church that was born of the Spirit that day was a prophetic church: prophecy was forever embedded in its very DNA. There is a great need for today's church to reconnect with this foundational truth: we need to know who we really are and live out of our identity. We need to have a Pentecost mindset and fully embrace the fact that we are children of outpouring and prophecy.

A central reality of the new covenant is that God has poured out his Spirit on his covenant people. He's poured out the very essence of who he is on us. He's not given us something superfluous or lightweight; he's given us the central core of his being, he's given us his best. Almighty God now dwells in the inmost being of every believer.

> *"Whoever believes in me, as Scripture has said, rivers of living water will flow from within them." By this he meant the Spirit, whom those who believed in him were later to receive.*
> John 7:38-39

> *But whoever is united with the Lord is one with him in spirit.*
> 1 Corinthians 6:17

To really appreciate the significance of this, we only have to look back to the Old Testament times. Under the old covenant the Holy Spirit was around and at work, but he was on particular people in particular places for a particular purpose.

I like this example from Judges 14:6:

> *The Spirit of the Lord came upon Samson in power so that he tore the lion apart with his bare hands....*

Samson experienced what it was like to encounter the manifest presence and power of the Holy Spirit, but under the old covenant this was a relatively rare occurrence: the Spirit was not yet given to **all** God's people. The Old Testament prophets caught glimpses of a future time of outpouring, such as Ezekiel 36:26-27, and of course Joel 2. John the Baptist, the last of the old covenant prophets, said these words:

> *"I baptise with water but after me will come one who will baptise you with the Holy Spirit..."*

John saw prophetically into the new covenant and realised that something completely new - something that he couldn't offer - was about to be **poured out** and offered to all God's children.

Everything changed the day the Holy Spirit fell on those disciples at Pentecost. The Spirit of Almighty God was now given to every disciple of Jesus. One of the incredible wonders of the new covenant is that the Spirit is poured out on all believers. We are 'baptised' in the Spirit - fully immersed. Each of us has been filled to overflowing with the very essence of the Godhead.

Do we take this seriously? Do we live in the truth of this? Or does it remain an abstract theological concept? We need to have both a Pentecost mindset and a Pentecost practice. We need to know and live out this fundamental truth. So what does this core reality of the new covenant actually look like for us? How does it affect how we live our lives? And what implications does it have for how we understand prophecy?

1. The Holy Spirit is a person

Firstly, the Holy Spirit is not an impersonal force. He's not an 'it'. He's a person, part of the Trinity with the Father and the Son, with his own personality and attributes.

It's so important that we don't treat him as a utility rather than a real person, asking for some heat or power or refreshment but ignoring him the rest of the time. He's a person – he's God – he's God with us. He's God abiding in us and with us. That's why Jesus could say to his disciples in John 16:7:

> "It's better for you that I leave. If I don't the friend won't come. But if I go I'll send him to you." [The Message]

Jesus is in heaven, seated at the right hand of the Father. But he has not abandoned us – he has given us *another Counsellor to be with us forever.* This *Parakletos* is the personification of the Father and the Son. He's the indwelling, empowering presence of God. And we can get to know him, and relate to him, as a real living person.

A key aspect of discipleship is pursuing knowledge and experience of each member of the Trinity. Most of us would say that we know Jesus pretty well; and the wealth of great teaching in recent years has led to many of us encountering the Father in significant ways. But how many of us would say that we really **knew** the Holy Spirit? My personal testimony is that getting to know the person of the Holy Spirit is one of the most significant and life-changing things I've ever done. And it's not that hard! He doesn't impose himself on us, but he does respond whenever we actively seek him out. He is waiting to be known.

2. Friendship with the Holy Spirit

Not only can we get to know the Holy Spirit as a person, but we are also invited into close fellowship and friendship with him. At the end of 2 Corinthians, Paul writes a simple sentence that summarises the ministry of the Trinity: *May the grace of our Lord Jesus Christ, and the love of God, and the fellowship of the Holy Spirit be with you all.* This is echoed in Philippians 2:1 where he relates the perfect relationship we can know with the Godhead to the sort of relationships we should have with our fellow believers, and Paul again uses the phrase *fellowship of the Spirit.*

The Holy Spirit is the one who 'fellowships' with us, who gives us connectedness with God on the inside. The deepest part of me – my spirit – is connected to the deepest part of God – his Spirit. And our inheritance as children of the new covenant is that we can cultivate an intentional friendship with the Holy Spirit who lives in us.

What incredible joy! What an amazing inheritance! To be friends with the Holy Spirit! This sacred friendship must never be based on what we can get out of him – we pursue friendship for no other reason than loving relationship. After all we don't develop friendships for what we can get out of people. Instead we give eternal thanks that we have a friend who will never leave us or forsake us, and treasure the gift that this friendship is to us.

Being friends with the Holy Spirit is about walking with him daily. In Galatians 5:16 Paul exhorts us to walk by the Spirit, and then promises us that if we do this *You will not gratify the desires of the flesh*. Walking with the Spirit in close fellowship with him gives us the power to follow the path of righteousness. It's the Spirit who has the power to overcome fleshly desires. As we become friends with him, and walk with him, we start to see his nature become manifest in our lives: deep joy, perfect peace, infinite goodness.

> *The fruit of the Spirit is love, joy, peace, forbearance, kindness, goodness, faithfulness, gentleness and self-control. Against such things there is no law.*
> Galatians 5:22-23

How do we walk with the Holy Spirit? By talking to him and listening to him; talking to him like a real person. The more we talk to him, the more he will draw us into conversation, and the more we will develop a sensitivity to his presence and voice. As we direct our attention towards him, we experience the world from his perspective: we learn his ways and we see what he sees. Our minds become synced with his:

> *Those who live according to the flesh have their minds set on what the flesh desires; but those who live in accordance with the Spirit have their minds set on what the Spirit desires. The mind governed by the flesh is death, but the mind governed by the Spirit is life and peace.*
> Romans 8:5-6

God wants us to know his Spirit to the degree that we know our closest friend.

> *But you know him, for he lives with you and will be in you.*
> John 14:17

3. Abundance and overflowing

A vital aspect of having a Pentecost mindset is an expectation of abundance in respect to the presence and power of the Holy Spirit. After all, so many of the words and phrases associated with him in the Bible are of the exuberant kind: *Poured out, Rivers of living water, How much more...* A poverty mindset expects a limited and rationed portion; a Pentecost mindset eagerly awaits the abundant generosity of heaven.

*"Which of you fathers, if your son asks for a fish, will give him a snake instead? Or if he asks for an egg, will give him a scorpion? If you then, though you are evil, know how to give good gifts to your children, **how much more** will your Father in heaven give the Holy Spirit to those who ask him!"*
Luke 11:11-13

We can never have too much of the presence of the Holy Spirit. We can have too much of lots of good things – food, wine, even water – but there is never 'too much' of the Holy Spirit. There are no toxic levels of his presence. It is only our own narrow expectations that limit his presence and power in our lives.

The same Spirit that empowered Jesus is at work in us and we need to be expectant of all that he can do in and through us. Let's start to see ourselves from Jesus' perspective:

"Whoever believes in me, as Scripture has said, rivers of living water will flow from within them."
John 7:38

4. Dependence

Part of learning to fellowship with the Holy Spirit, and to become friends with him, is about learning to depend on him. Jesus modelled this life of dependency on the Spirit; he modelled for us what it looks like to be completely led by, surrendered to, and empowered by the Holy Spirit.

Jesus returned to Galilee in the power of the Spirit, and news about him spread through the whole countryside.
Luke 4:14

Jesus chose to be fully man when he came to earth from heaven. He could have done it all by himself, but rather than being reliant on his divine attributes, he chose to be completely dependent on the Holy Spirit's anointing and empowerment. And this is why Jesus could say to his followers that they would do even greater things than he had done, because post-Pentecost, every believer has the unlimited potential of the Holy Spirit's anointing:

"Very truly I tell you, whoever believes in me will do the works I have been doing, and they will do even greater things than these, because I am going to the Father."
John 14:12

The gospels are an invitation to have the same ministry in the Spirit that Jesus had. Jesus was not just filled with the Spirit, but chose to be led by the Spirit, and it's the same journey for us. A Pentecost mindset is not simply focused on the Spirit's empowerment, but on the daily choice to follow the Spirit and depend on him. Life in the Spirit is about being led by the Spirit (Romans 8:14, Galatians 5:18).

To follow his leadership means trusting him and being attentive to his promptings. We cultivate an awareness of how he wants to lead us – in both the small everyday things as well as the big things. We submit our thoughts, words and deeds to him. We honour him as the Spirit of wisdom and revelation whose job it is to reveal the Father and Jesus to us. And as we constantly look to him and interact with him, our focus shifts from ourselves to God, and we become people who are able to perceive the kingdom of God around us.

Since we live by the Spirit, let us keep in step with the Spirit
Galatians 5:25

Relationship is the Key

We've seen how the Holy Spirit is a person that we can relate to; and how we are invited into deep fellowship with him; that we can expect an abundance of his presence and power; and how Jesus modelled a lifestyle of dependence on him. How does this Pentecost mindset affect our approach to hearing God and moving in prophetic gifts?

Hearing God is all about relationship; and the most significant relationship for prophecy is the one we have with the Holy Spirit. To grow in hearing God and in prophetic gifts we have to grow in knowledge of the person of the Holy Spirit, who is the very essence of truth and revelation.

As we welcome the presence and friendship of our remarkable *Parakletos*, something wonderful starts to happen – rather than prophecy being something that we 'do', it begins to change into a natural overflow of a deepening friendship. As we walk and talk with our *Parakletos* he shares his heart with us, he shows us where he's at work in the world around us, he lets us see people with the eyes of Jesus, he connects us to the very heartbeat of our heavenly Father.

The truth we all need to get hold of, and then live out, is that we can get to know the Holy Spirit as a close personal friend; and as we do that the prophetic will grow. We pursue friendship with him first – and prophecy will be a fruit that comes from that friendship.

A mindset of abundance allows us to truly expect a full measure of his presence, gifts and revelation. We don't need to strive to hear God, or worry that there is not enough anointing to go round. If God has **poured out** his Spirit upon us, then we can be confident that his voice will always be accessible to us.

And finally, perhaps most significantly for anyone committed to follow the methodology of Jesus, a growing dependence on the Spirit will send us out into the world. He is not content to leave us where we are; his intention is to make us more like Jesus so that we can be carriers of the revelation of Jesus to those who don't yet know him. Being dependent on the Holy Spirit means surrendering to his leadership in all aspects of our lives. He is the ultimate prophetic missionary and his goal for us is to send us out on the mission of Jesus. Ultimately, life in the Spirit is not about asking, *"What can you do for us?"* but rather asking, *"**What can we do for you?**"*

Chapter 8

The Revelation of the Trinity

We can think of revelation in many different ways. In the previous chapter we met the Person who *is* revelation, and in the next chapter we'll look at how he brings revelation to us. But in this chapter I want to look at how the concept of revelation is actually at the heart of both the gospel and the narrative of God reaching out to a broken world.

The story of God's relationship with mankind is one of both revelation and hiddeness. In the creation story we glimpse a time when the connection between humans and their Creator was pure and untarnished. But then darkness came, and with it, concealment. People hid themselves from God and sin blinded them from the truth. Spiritual reality became hard to fathom, and the flow of revelation from God to man was hindered. God didn't stop communicating with his people, but after the Fall there was now so much to distract them from pursuing the clear certainty of his voice and presence. Mankind stopped listening.

There is an interesting paradox in the Bible: the God who is committed to revelation, described in Daniel 2:29 as the *revealer of mysteries*, often chooses to communicate with his people in a veiled manner through riddles and parables. He seems to have a preference for symbolism and metaphor. Numbers 12:6-8 indicates his chosen methodology:

> *The Lord said, "Listen to my words: When there is a prophet among you, I, the Lord, reveal myself to them in visions, I*

speak to them in dreams. But this is not true of my servant Moses; he is faithful in all my house. With him I speak face to face, clearly and not in riddles; he sees the form of the Lord."

Moses was the only person God spoke to in such a clear manner; with the other prophets it was through a much more symbolic and mysterious medium. When we look at the ministry of Jesus we see that he did most of his teaching through parables. Jesus' tactic was to partially hide the truth from his listeners so that only those with a real hunger for God and his righteousness would be able to gain understanding.

> *"I speak to them in parables: though seeing they do not see; though hearing they do not hear or understand…. But blessed are your eyes because they see, and your ears because they hear."*
> Matthew 13:13,16

Moses was a man who was marked by his humility. In Numbers 12:3 it says that he was more humble than anyone else on the face of the earth. And it is this one man whom the Lord spoke clearly to, in an unveiled manner. By examining both the story of Moses, and the gospels, we find that it is those with humility and a child-like faith who are able to grasp the truth God is revealing. God looks for those who are seeking him, and he can be found by those who seek him with all their heart. He is committed to revealing his truth to those who hunger to encounter him, but hides himself from the spiritually proud and self-righteous:

> *At the time Jesus said, "I praise you, Father, Lord of heaven and earth, because you have hidden these things from the wise and learned, and revealed them to little children."*
> Matthew 11:25

Faith and humility are the keys for accessing revelation that God holds out to us. For those with eyes to see, and a heart of faith, revelation has never been too inaccessible. God has always revealed himself through creation:

> *The heavens declare the glory of God; the skies proclaim*

the work of his hands. Day after day they pour forth speech; night after night they reveal knowledge.
Psalm 19:1-2

Similarly, the unveiled truth of the nature of God is everywhere – but we have to have eyes to see.

There's an interesting parallel to this in modern cosmology. Cosmic background radiation is radiation that fills the universe and can be detected everywhere in space. It is the afterglow of the Big Bang and unveils the reality of the moment of creation. But until the 1960s physicists had no idea it was there. It is invisible to the naked eye and can only be detected through radio telescopes, but once scientist realised it existed they found that it came from every direction in space.

Like cosmic background radiation, the revelation of God is everywhere, but we have to intentionally seek it – with eyes of faith and a heart of humility.

And revelation is at the heart of the gospel: in particular the revelation of the three persons of the Trinity. The glorious truth that is now unveiled to us is that God is not an abstract concept or distant entity. The Creator has come among us to reveal to us who he is; within the unity of the Godhead there is a community of three persons:

- our heavenly Father who loves us unconditionally
- Jesus our Saviour, the light of the world, through whom we have eternal life
- the Holy Spirit, our friend and helper, who dwells in our innermost being

The gospels contain within them the unveiling – the making known – of the Trinity, and through it, God's plan of salvation. This three-part personhood is unveiled to the world at Jesus' baptism, where *Heaven was opened, and he saw the Spirit of God descending like a dove and alighting on him. And a voice from heaven said, "This is my Son, whom I love; with him I am well pleased."* (Matthew 3:16-17)

Here is the Father speaking identity to his Son, and the Holy Spirit coming to dwell with him. With the Trinity we get the picture of a perfect three-way relationship of pure and eternal love. This is the God whom we adore and worship. And this is the revelation we take to the world around us.

The ultimate goal of prophetic ministry is to reveal who God is; to reveal the truth of the nature of God to those who cannot yet see him. To reveal that they have a Father in heaven who loves them; to unveil Jesus their Saviour to them; and to introduce them to the Holy Spirit who will never leave them. From this perspective we see how prophecy and mission are so interconnected. Yes, a simple definition of prophecy is to communicate what God is saying; but a more profound way of looking at prophecy is to think of it in terms of holding out reality so that it can be clearly seen. Prophecy is fundamentally about revealing truth that is hidden, so that people can see and hear. And the greatest truth that we can ever reveal to people is that God is real and loves them.

Prophecy Reveals the Father

Jesus came to this earth for many important reasons, but a primary reason was to reveal the Father and give us a true picture of what he is like. Jesus came to be the visible manifestation of the invisible God:

> *No one has ever seen God, but the one and only Son, who is himself God and is in closest relationship with the Father, has made him known.*
> John 1:18

Jesus was the most prophetic person who ever lived on this earth because he revealed to us who the Father is, and what his relationship with him is like. And he did it in such a perfect way that he could say, *"Anyone who has seen me has seen the Father."* (John 14:9).

Jesus' revelation of the Father is the greatest and most profound revelation – the greatest prophecy – of all time. But as disciples of Jesus we get to join in as well. Engaging with prophetic ministry is a really important way in which we can follow in Jesus' footsteps – when we realise that true prophecy is simply accessing and revealing the Father's heart and nature. We can engage with prophecy in such a way that we reveal the Father through it. And it doesn't get much better than that.

There are two aspects of revealing the Father through prophecy:

1. Prophecy represents his nature

True prophecy will carry with it the nature of the Father – both in content and in conduct. We can represent the goodness, kindness and generosity of God, both with the words that we speak over people, and the way we speak them (the way we conduct our ministry). It's important when we prophesy that we remember that we are representing our perfect heavenly Father and so we speak in a loving, gracious manner to people. We certainly don't yell at them!

If we take a holistic view of the prophetic we could say that whenever we are faithfully representing the nature of the Father by our words and actions, then we are being prophetic. So if we speak words that represent the Father's incredible kindness towards people, and if through those words someone gets to see something of the kindness of God, then we are being prophetic, even though we may not label it as 'prophecy' in the narrowest sense of the word. Any time we are representing the Father and revealing his nature we are embracing the prophetic call on the church.

In order to faithfully represent the Father through prophecy we have to be hungry for words that communicate the goodness of God. We have to intentionally lean into his nature, sense his goodness, and from that place be eager to prophesy words that reveal the essence of his glorious being. We also have to choose to see people as God sees them, to not look at them as the world does, but to have the eyes of the Father. The very heart of prophecy is to look at people as the Father looks at them and to speak to them as he would speak to them.

2. Prophecy connects us to the Father's heart

Prophecy is more than just giving someone a word. It's about sharing the Father's heart with them so that they can be drawn deeper into relationship with him, so that they can discover more about who he is. It's about connecting people to his heart so that our hearts beat in time with his. As Mike Bickle says, *"We prophesy each time we make known his passionate heart."*[8] There is a call on all prophetic people to explore the Father's heart for everyone we meet and then speak out the revelation we find there.

One of the reasons I absolutely love being involved in prophetic ministry is because I get to see what's in the very heart of God for people and see his amazing passion for them. There have been many times when I have been overwhelmed with what I've seen in the Father's heart when I'm prophesying over people. It's an amazing privilege to connect people with the heart of their heavenly Father through a word of prophecy – so that when you have finished prophesying over someone they are closer to the heart of the Father.

The ministry of prophecy has the potential to call people to walk out the first commandment as passionate lovers of God, as it connects them to the Father's heart. It motivates believers to stir up their first love. As they connect with God's heart through prophetic ministry, their own hearts are growing deeper and deeper in love with God. Whenever we reach out and touch God's heart we find our own hearts will grow and be more filled with the Father's love.

Prophetic people need to be people of the heart. To grow in the prophetic is to grow in passion for God's heart, to desire to find out what is on his heart, to communicate his heart, and to minister from that place. As prophetic people we need to be living from the heart of God, and our ministry needs to flows out of experiencing the Father's heart:

- so that we can love as he loves
- so that we can pray as he is praying
- so that we can see what he is doing and go and join in
- so that we can represent his heart

Sometimes God calls us to journey deep into his heart to the extent that we start to feel as he feels. We may feel his compassion, zeal, grief, affection or joy. Jeremiah is a good example of a prophet in the

[8] Mike Bickle - *Growing in the Prophetic* (Lake Mary: Charisma House, 2008), 70

Bible who was given the privilege of feeling what God felt. When we read the pages of Jeremiah we can sense the raw emotion from the heart of God whose people had turned their backs on him. I believe that Jeremiah experienced the emotions of God to the extent that it was a significant burden for him to carry – the burden of God's heart. We hear the heartbreak of God through the message Jeremiah had to bear:

> "I remember the devotion of your youth, how as a bride you loved me and followed me through the wilderness... What fault did your ancestors find in me, that they strayed so far from me?... Has a nation ever changed its gods? But my people have exchanged their Glory for worthless idols. Be appalled at this, O heavens, and shudder with great horror," declares the Lord... "Does a young woman forget her jewellery, a bride her wedding ornaments? Yet my people have forgotten me, days without number."
> Jeremiah 2:1,5,11,32

It's personal; it's heart-rending. We can only begin to imagine how Jeremiah would have felt as he was given the responsibility of carrying such words.

So we need to acknowledge that sometimes our pursuit of God's heart may cause us to encounter some strong emotions. But whatever the journey looks like we need to be meditating, pursuing, being consumed with the heart and nature of God. And we need to be asking ourselves whether we are representing God's heart and nature with our words and actions.

From a practical point of view, here are three great questions to ask the Father whenever we are praying for, or prophesying over, someone:

- *What aspect of your nature do you want to reveal to this person today?*
- *What is on your heart for this person today?*
- *How can I prophesy a revelation of your heart?*

Prophecy Reveals Jesus

We've seen how prophecy reveals the Father. But prophecy is also about the revelation of Jesus. There is one prophet in the Bible who was given the highest of callings: to witness to the Light of the World. His name was John the Baptist. Jesus describes John as the 'greatest' of the old covenant prophets. He was the prophet that revealed Jesus Christ, the Son of God, to the world.

> *There was a man sent from God whose name was John. He came as a witness to testify concerning that light, so that through him all might believe.*
> John 1:6-7

The ministry of John the Baptist was to testify – bear witness – to Jesus, and to prepare the way for him.

> *The next day John saw Jesus coming towards him and said, "Look, the Lamb of God, who takes away the sin of the world!"*
> John 1:29

> *"I have seen and I testify that this is the Son of God."*
> John 1:34

It is John's testimony that Jesus is the Son of God, and the manner in which this prepared the way for Jesus, that makes him the greatest of the old covenant prophets. And this reminds us that a primary aspect of prophecy is to reveal and bear witness to Jesus. We find further evidence for this in the writings of the other John of the New Testament – John the Apostle's book of Revelation.

The book of Revelation is all about the revelation and the testimony of Jesus. Right at the beginning of the book of Revelation John sees a revelation of Jesus in his glory and majesty. And then in chapter 19 John describes an encounter he had with an angel:

> *At this I fell at his feet to worship him. But he said to me, "Do not do it! I am a fellow servant with you and with your brothers who hold to the testimony of Jesus. Worship God! For the testimony of Jesus is the spirit of prophecy."*
> Revelation 19:10

The word translated as 'spirit' in this verse means 'essence'. The angel's words tell us that the most profound prophetic word or experience is one that carries with it a revelation of Jesus:

- the essence of prophecy is to behold Jesus in our midst and bear witness to all that he is and does
- the essence of prophecy is to attest to the truth of Jesus and draw people to him
- the essence of prophecy is to reveal Jesus' heart and will for his people

As we reveal Jesus to people – as we testify about him and bear witness about him – this is the very essence and 'spirit' of prophecy, the ultimate prophetic expression. Prophecy is many different things but I believe that at its very heart it is designed to unfold the glory, majesty and beauty of Jesus.

And the challenge for all of us operating in the prophetic is this: does this prophecy that I am speaking contain in some way a testimony, a revelation, of Jesus? Is this prophecy leading people to Jesus? Is it unveiling Jesus to them?

The Spirit Reveals the Father and the Son

In the previous chapter we've already looked at how the Holy Spirit is so closely tied to prophecy. He is the Revealer. He reveals truth to us; in fact his name is 'Truth'. He searches out the deep, hidden things of God and makes them known to us. Through the in-dwelling Spirit we have direct communion with God and can hear his voice.

His greatest gift to us is the revelation of the Father and Jesus:

- it's through him that we have a revelation of the Fatherhood of God:

  The Spirit you received brought about your adoption to sonship. And by him we cry, "Abba, Father." The Spirit himself testifies with our spirit that we are God's children.
  Romans 8:15-16

- it's through the Spirit's ministry in our lives that we are able to have a revelation of the Lordship of Jesus and know him as the Son of God:

  No one can say, "Jesus is Lord," except by the Holy Spirit.
  1 Corinthians 12:3

- the Spirit gives us assurance of our new life in God's love:

  God has put his Spirit in our hearts as a deposit, guaranteeing what is to come.
  2 Corinthians 1:22

  This is how we know that we live in him and he in us: he has given us of his Spirit.
  1 John 4:13

- and we grow in knowledge of God through him:

  I keep asking that the God of our Lord Jesus Christ, the glorious Father, may give you the Spirit of wisdom and revelation, so that you may know him better.
  Ephesians 1:17

The Holy Spirit takes the thoughts, heart and intentions of the Father and the Son and makes them known to us. He delights to give us ever-increasing revelation of the love of the Father and the glory of Jesus. And he works through disciples to reveal the Father and the Son to the world around us. He goes ahead of us and prepares hearts and minds, so that lost sheep are made ready to receive the revelation of the Father and the Son that we bring to them.

Chapter 9

Different Types of Revelation

Having spent some time looking at the 'Who' of revelation, we are now going to turn our attention to the 'how', and consider the different forms revelation can take.

The Holy Spirit is the most creative person in the universe and can bring revelation to us in many different ways. However both the Bible and experience suggest that there are a few broad categories of prophetic revelation; and as we unpack what it really looks like to hear the voice of our Good Shepherd it can be incredibly helpful to spend some time examining each of these different types.

From a practical point of view, and as I've worked with and mentored many people over the years, it's the case that different people receive different types of revelation from the Holy Spirit. So for most of us, we'll be particularly tuned in to one or two forms of revelation, which will come fairly naturally to us; other types of revelation may be much more uncommon. To grow in prophecy we first of all acknowledge where we are strong, and then press in for breakthrough where we are weak.

I believe that it's helpful to think in terms of five general categories of revelation:

1. Scripture

By this I mean the Holy Spirit impressing on you a particular verse or passage from the Bible. So you may be reading the Bible and a certain bit of it jumps out at you, and you know that the Holy Spirit is speaking into your life there and then through that verse or passage. In those words on the page God reveals something new to you or brings truth in a fresh way. Or you may be praying for someone and all of a sudden a verse pops into your head and you realise that God wants to encourage the person through that particular bit of scripture. You may even hear God speak the reference (i.e. book, chapter and verse) to you.

I like this kind of revelation because it's usually fairly clear-cut and straightforward, and it reminds us that the more time we spend studying and feeding on God's written word, the more he will use it to speak to us prophetically. All revelation needs to be grounded in, and birthed from, the written word of God.

2. Hearing

'Hearing' is revelation that comes in the form of words, phrases or sentences. There are very many examples throughout the Bible of people 'hearing the word of the Lord', though we're not often told what that was actually like for the people involved.

When Jesus got baptised at the start of his ministry there was an audible voice from heaven; his Father declaring Jesus' identity as his Son:

> And a voice from heaven said, "This is my Son, whom I love; with him I am well pleased."
> Matthew 3:7

And in Acts 9 we read about Saul hearing the voice of Jesus in the momentous conversion experience on the road to Damascus:

> He fell to the ground and heard a voice say to him, "Saul, Saul, why do you persecute me?"
> Acts 9:4

I know a number of people (including my father-in-law) who themselves have heard the audible voice of God, which has been an incredibly significant experience for them. However much more common is the internal voice, when God speaks his words to our minds and hearts. So a word, a phrase or a sentence suddenly alights in our mind, as though the Holy Spirit is talking directly to our thoughts from within.

Sometimes this voice can seem very loud to us, even though it's happening on the inside – the words really resound in our minds. At other times the voice is as quiet as a gentle whisper, so soft that we can easily miss it or dismiss it as one of our own thoughts.

I'm sometimes asked why God chooses to speak in such a quiet voice at times. I believe he mostly speaks in whispers because he is so committed to relationship with us that he wants us to lean in close. When someone is speaking very quietly we have no option but to get very near to them, and concentrate hard on what they are saying if we don't want to miss any of their words. It's the same with God.

As we journey deeper into the prophetic we have to learn to recognise God's voice, so even if it comes to us as the quietest whisper our spirits will be attuned to it. Jesus is confident that we will:

> His sheep follow him because they know his voice. But they will never follow a stranger; in fact they will run away from him because they do not recognise a stranger's voice.
> John 10:4-5

The truth is that:

- learning to recognise God's voice takes time and practice – but Jesus promises us we will be able to distinguish between his voice and anyone else's voice
- we need to trust the Lord's ability to lead us more than the enemy's ability to deceive us

Recognition takes time and flows out of relationship. The closer we grow to the Lord the more we will be able to recognise his voice. The more we fix our eyes on Jesus, the more clearly we will hear him.

I'm now fairly good at distinguishing God's voice from my own thoughts, but I'm still learning. A great way to practice prophetic listening is to journal. Find some space and quiet where you can sit down and engage with God; spend some time worshipping and welcoming the presence of the Holy Spirit; and then start writing. Don't analyse what it is you are writing, just let the flow of words get on the page. You may find it helpful to ask God questions such as, *"What do you want to say to me today?"* The idea is that God responds to your thoughts and questions and the two-way conversation is captured on paper.

3. Seeing

In this type of revelation God communicates with us through pictures and visions. Daniel and Ezekiel were Old Testament prophets who received visions. As it says in Daniel 10:1:

> *In the third year of Cyrus king of Persia, a revelation was given to Daniel. Its message was true and it concerned a great war. The understanding of the message came to him in a vision.*

An example from the New Testament is in Acts 10 when Peter has a vision:

> *About noon the following day as they were on their journey and approaching the city, Peter went up on the roof to pray. He became hungry and wanted something to eat, and while the meal was being prepared, he fell into a trance. He saw heaven opened and something like a large sheet being let down to earth by its four corners. It contained all kinds of four-footed animals, as well as reptiles and birds. Then a voice told him, "Get up, Peter. Kill and eat."*

When the Holy Spirit brings revelation to us in the form of visions and pictures it is usually an internal process, and we perceive the content through our 'mind's eye'. Occasionally people may have what could be described as an 'open-eye' vision, and they will see the vision as clearly as in the natural. These experiences are quite rare, though, and rather than spending time trying to work out the particular category of vision it's much more important that we pay careful attention to what God is communicating to us through the picture or vision.

Of course the big question is, *"How do I know it's God, and not something I've made up from my imagination?"* It's often a question of practice and learning to recognise the particular quality of God-given pictures. A couple of useful questions to ask are:

- what is the impact the picture leaves on my spirit?
- does the picture bring me into the presence of God?

Sometimes the simplest prophetic pictures can carry significant revelation, and so-called 'cheesy' clichés can turn out to be really profound. Just last week I was doing a prophetic exercise with three other people and the Holy Spirit gave each of us, independently, a picture of a waterfall. Waterfalls are high up in the cliché ratings, but God spoke so clearly and powerfully to each of us through our different waterfall pictures, and it was a reminder to me that with prophetic pictures we have to simply receive them by faith, regardless of how hackneyed they may seem.

My advice with prophetic pictures is not to get too analytical with them – they are simply a conversation between you and God. It's more about allowing the Holy Spirit to take you deeper into a picture and maintaining that relationship with him, rather than try to work out what it all means. Remember, receiving revelation is always about relationship, not task. If we're not careful we can get too task-focussed, concentrating on a problem to be solved, and losing sight of the relational aspect of all prophetic experiences.

If possible, if time allows, don't jump too quickly to the interpretation. Rather than receiving the picture and then asking straight away, *"What does it mean?"*, pause a while and allow the Holy Spirit to lead you deeper into the revelation. There is a real joy to be found in exploring prophetic pictures and visions with the Holy Spirit. Let him take you by the hand and go on a journey of discovery into all that you are seeing. Enjoy simply dwelling in the revelation a while.

4. Sensing

Under this heading would come discernment, intuition, burdens, impressions, vibes and gut feelings. That 'just knowing' awareness that is so hard to explain. Sometimes we can also experience actual physical sensations and emotional sensations given to us by the Holy Spirit: in these situations God is speaking to us by letting us feel his emotions towards a person or by letting us feel the emotions or pain of others.

It's important to recognise 'sensing' as a valid form of prophetic revelation; in fact for a number of highly prophetic people I know, this is the main way they receive revelation from the Holy Spirit.

Sensing is an important type of revelation to receive in the **activity** of our lives – my experience is that for many people words and pictures come to them in their quiet times with God, but sensing is the way they hear God as they go about their daily lives. And if this is the case then we all need to pay careful attention to those promptings, impressions and 'feelings' we get in the busyness of life.

Sometimes God brings us specific warnings through a sense that something is wrong. Here is an example from my friend Ceri:

> *Before my daughter was due to go to Canada I kept getting a sense or gut feeling that I needed to pray for her protection and provision, particularly whilst driving.*
>
> *One evening whilst she was away that same feeling came back and I prayed the same prayer. The next day that feeling hadn't left me. Instinctively I knew something was wrong. Together with my husband we prayed for my daughter's protection and provision throughout the day. At 3pm I received news that she'd been involved in a car crash. Whilst on a very isolated stretch of road the driver had lost control, hit some rocks, leaving the road and ending up in a ravine. My shock at the news quickly turned to thanksgiving as I heard how, despite the severity of the crash, they walked away unscathed. Additionally, another motorist passed (unusual for that stretch of road) and gave assistance. I was so thankful that I'd paid attention to my gut instinct and was able to cover the situation in prayer.*

5. Dreams

I'll be really honest with you here – prophetic dreams are extremely rare for me. Fortunately I know plenty of people who do get prophetic dreams and have learnt a lot from their experiences.

Of course dreams are a very valid way for us to receive revelation; the Bible has many stories about God speaking to people in dreams. One of my favourite examples is in chapter 16 of Acts:

> They went to Phrygia, and then on through the region of Galatia. Their plan was to turn west into Asia province, but the Holy Spirit blocked that route. So they went to Mysia and tried to go north to Bithynia, but the Spirit of Jesus wouldn't let them go there either. Proceeding on through Mysia, they went down to the seaport Troas. That night Paul had a dream: A Macedonian stood on the far shore and called across the sea, "Come over to Macedonia and help us!" The dream gave Paul his map. (The Message)

Most of us will have countless dreams through the course of our lives, but the majority of them will be ordinary ones which are simply a way for the brain to process information and occur during REM (rapid eye movement) sleep. They tend to be stimulated by our environment or recent events, and we often forget them soon after waking.

Prophetic dreams from the Lord have a special quality to them and are much more memorable. We have to learn to discern which of our dreams are from God, in the same way that we learn to discern his voice, and we can do this by praying about significant dreams we receive and keeping a written record of them.

Interpreting prophetic dreams is a spiritual gift, and has to be done prayerfully. We can only receive interpretation through revelation given by the Holy Spirit, so if you think God has given you a prophetic dream ask him what it means. Listen carefully to him and don't be tempted to use symbolism or formulas. There is not a formula or dream dictionary that will tell you what your dream means; it has to come through relationship with the Holy Spirit.

Personal Stories

I'm a great believer in unpacking spiritual language and concepts so that we get to the 'nitty-gritty' of what is actually going on – I find this helps people really grasp things, minimises misconceptions, and enables people to effectively apply the theory to their own contexts. So here are three examples of the 'mechanics' of receiving revelation, firstly from my own experience, then from my friends John and Joanne, both of whom are experienced practitioners.

Most of the time when I receive revelation the process works something like this:

I first of all receive a prophetic picture, which emerges rather than popping into my head fully-formed – I may start off seeing a small part of it, or it may start off as one thing and then change slightly. What I've learned over the years is that *I must resist the urge to dismiss the revelation at this stage because it doesn't make sense*. Rather I need to stay in a place of faith and receptivity, patiently waiting for the revelation to emerge. Sometimes it will be a still picture, like a photograph; at other times it will be a moving picture, like a film.

Once I've received the fully formed prophetic picture there will be a witness in my spirit (a sense of, *"that's right"*) that what I'm seeing is from the Lord, so I give thanks for the picture and press in for more. I'll pay careful attention to aspects of the picture that the Holy Spirit is highlighting for me, and be careful not to start striving to work out what it may mean.

At this stage I usually find that I start to receive more revelation in the form of 'sensing' – I'll start to get a gut feeling about what God is saying through the picture, or I may sense a particular emotion that brings an added dimension.

The final stage is usually 'hearing', when a word or phrase pops into my head, with an accompanying resonance in my spirit, which gives me greater understanding of the interpretation of the picture.

This is how my friend John receives revelation:

> *When God starts to speak to me it usually comes in the form of a few words that I see in my mind's eye: they look like words as if I am reading a sentence, but it's just the beginning of a sentence. I often hear the words as well.*

As I start to speak out the words that I can see, I get the rest of the sentence, and then further sentences. I don't necessarily see the new (hidden) words; they just come as I begin to speak the few words that I have already seen. It is stepping out into the unknown, but the Lord is faithful. I go with what I have been shown, and the rest comes. I have learnt to recognize when the revelation ceases, and so I will just stop speaking when the words stop (though there is of course the temptation to keep on speaking!).

At a number of significant times in my life I have heard the audible voice of God. For example, in 1994, six weeks before the Toronto Blessing made a significant impact on the church that I was leading, the Lord audibly told me that in a short period of time I would see the Holy Spirit moving in extraordinary ways on and through people – ways that I would have never imagined. The voice was in conjunction with my looking at a pool whose surface was being disturbed by lots of insects skimming the surface. There were lots of ripples all over surface. So, when everything happened six weeks later, I wasn't surprised. The Lord had prepared me. At other times, when I have had to make big church decisions, lead out in faith (and often feeling very vulnerable), the Lord has spoken audibly to me which has been incredibly encouraging. When he speaks to me in this way the clarity is extraordinary. It is like two people sitting down or walking together and just chatting away.

This is how my friend Joanne receives revelation:

I really love praying and find that God speaks most clearly to me as I pray. So if I'm in a situation where I want to prophesy over someone, I will start to pray in tongues. This helps me to focus my attention on God and tune in to the flow of the Holy Spirit. I can sense the connection of my spirit with the Holy Spirit. After a while God will give me some prophetic words for the person I'm praying for, but it comes straight out of my mouth, by-passing my mind. I'll often be surprised at the words I find myself speaking; in fact the challenge is to stop my mind questioning them and just trust the Spirit.

As I'm speaking out the word that God has given me he will often give me a clear prophetic picture that brings an added dimension to the revelation, as well as confirmation.

The Characteristics of God's Voice – How to Discern True Revelation

The question everyone asks when taking those first steps in prophecy is, *"How do I know it's God and not just me?"*

When the Holy Spirit brings us revelation it will have certain characteristics that help us discern God's voice from our own thoughts, emotions and imagination. It may be the subtlest impression from the Spirit – the gentlest of whispers – but if it's from God's heart we will be able to recognise it, because divine revelation has particular qualities.

- Revelation from God tends to be spontaneous, whereas thoughts from our own minds are usually analytical and follow a logical path. When we are thinking with our rational, human minds, it's usually the case that one thought follows another. However a good indication that God is speaking to us is that something spontaneously lands in our heads or hearts that has no connection to our previous train of thoughts. Of course that doesn't guarantee that it is from God, but we should at least pay attention to it because it may be revelation from the Holy Spirit.

  I clearly remember an occasion a few years ago when I was in the middle of a great worship service at our church when out of nowhere I had a clear vision of footprints walking out of the back door and away from the building. I knew pretty much straight away that God was starting to call our family from one church base to another, within our network of churches. It took many months for us to properly process this call and to make that move; but what struck me was how spontaneous the initial revelation had been. I hadn't been thinking about moving base, it was not on my radar at all.

- Revelation from God has a special quality to it. Its content may be rather unexpected or unusual. It will be full of love and wisdom. Its tone will reflect the nature and character of our heavenly Father. When I hear God speak to me his voice is often accompanied with a sense of surprise and wonder: his revelation is more radical, more pure, more profound than anything I could come up with. His words are not ones I would normally think on my own.

- True revelation comes with a resonance, the spirit-to-spirit connection, when you 'just know because you just know.' The experience of this inner witness varies from person to person: sometimes we may hear, *"Yes, that's true"* or *"No, that's not right."* Others just seem to know instinctively. Some people experience an emotional or physical reaction that confirms that God is speaking to them, such as a faster heart rate or heat on their body. Very often we will know God's peace and rest when we are on the right path.

A Word of Warning

As we grow in our abilty to hear God's voice we have to beware of two things that often masquerade as revelation:

- **Idols in our heart**

An idol is anything other than God that we are worshipping, anything that is claiming too much of our attention and distracting us from our whole-hearted devotion to the Lord. When we hold things – be they objects, desires, or people – in over-high esteem it's easy to mistake the demanding and insistent voices of these idols for God's voice.

If you are idolising something, if you really want something, whether it's the latest iphone or a new house, then you are going to have problems discerning any revelation you may receive. Idols have loud voices and are quite clever as masquerading as the voice of God. If you are seeking God about a new purchase or new job, for example, it's important to first of all examine your heart and ensure that the thing you want hasn't supplanted the Lord as first in your devotions.

- **Our emotions**

Whereas one of the main aims in prophetic ministry is to live and minister from the Father's heart, this is not the same as ministering from our emotions. A mature prophet is someone who has learnt to distinguish between the two. Yes, we pursue and desire God's heart, and we may encounter the very emotions of God as we do that; but strong emotions are not always the same thing as prophetic revelation. Just because we are feeling a strong emotion does not mean we are in tune with what God is feeling.

It's really important that our hearts are on the same wavelength as the Lord's, rather than tuning in to other people's vulnerability and pain. If you are prophesying over someone and you intuitively perceive that they are carrying a lot of grief and brokenness, the danger is that you tune in to their emotions rather than tuning in to God's heart, and you end up prophesying from that place, or prophesying from your own emotions, rather than from a pure flow of the Holy Spirit's revelation. There is a real danger of attaching the adjective 'prophetic' to words which are basically just 'sympathy' words – words that come from human hearts.

In any situation where there are a lot of emotions involved we have to exercise extreme caution when seeking to hear from God. When someone that we love is in real need it's very easy to confuse the voice of our emotions with the voice of God. Many of us will have had situations where someone we are close to has been very ill, or in serious trouble, and we are desperate for the situation to be resolved. We can think we are hearing from God, but actually it's the voice of our emotions. In these kind of situations there is so much potential for harm. I know of terminally ill people receiving prophecies they were going to be healed, and childless couples receiving prophecies of babies, and in so many of these cases it turned out that these were emotions speaking rather than the Spirit of God.

If we are in an emotionally-charged environment then it's good to take our time as we ask God about the situation. We shouldn't rush to communicate what we think God is saying. Rather we should step back, and take time to tune into God's heart. It's so important that we can objectively ask him for his perspective, setting aside our own emotions and opinions, so that they do not interfere with our ability to hear his voice.

When Revelation Seems to be Negative

From time to time prophetic people may receive revelation that seems negative: they may perceive sin in someone's life, or the grief that someone is carrying. They may sense that God is speaking warning about a situation, or that he wants to bring correction to a person. How do we handle such revelation?

Firstly we need to be very cautious, and to always ask the Lord for wisdom as to the best way to proceed. Remember, there is **no rush** to deliver a prophecy, so with a 'heavy' word of warning or correction it is best to devote some time to carefully pray about it. I would also strongly recommend taking it to your church leaders, before sharing it with the person it's for, so that you are making yourself accountable.

From time to time the Holy Spirit may give you a word of knowledge – a specific piece of information – about someone, and the information you receive reveals something negative. So, for example, you may get revelation about a particular sin in someone's life. What's important to realise in situations like this is that the reason God is showing you the problem is because he wants you to **prophesy the solution**! It's usually the case that he doesn't intend for you to speak out the negative thing that you prophetically perceive; rather that you wait on God until he shows you his amazing solution to the issue, so that you can prophesy life over the person concerned and replace the negative with a positive. It's not the job of a prophet to convict people of sin – the Holy Spirit is perfectly capable of doing that without our help.

Growing in Revelation

I'll finish off this chapter by encouraging you that by far the best way to grow in revelation is by stepping out and practising. We can all be regularly asking the Holy Spirit to give us more, and he will, but we have to step out in faith and have a go in order to see the answer to our prayers. If you want to grow in hearing his voice, then practise careful listening the next time you are praying for someone. If you want to grow in prophetic pictures and visions, ask God for them and be prepared to share whatever hazy impressions you get. I like to think in terms of exercising our prophetic muscles: some of us have naturally big muscles, some of us have smaller ones, but the way to grow them is to exercise them – regularly and consistently!

Chapter 10

What do we do with Revelation?

Revelation, of course, is only the beginning. God speaks for a purpose and wants us to journey with him and our Christian community towards entering a complete fulfilment and realisation of his spoken word to us.

We can fill our lives with revelation, with all sorts of stunning, technicoloured dreams and visions. And believe me, I absolutely love this. But revelation is only a part of the prophetic process, it's just the beginning really. Mature followers of Jesus learn to take his words seriously and then act on them.

Weighing

The first thing we have to do with revelation is to weigh it carefully. Most prophecies we hear and speak will not be 100% accurate and infallible. Some may come very close, but at the end of the day it's still a human vessel trying to communicate the very mind of God using contemporary language, and we will always need a healthy dose of realism and humility to properly discern what God is actually saying. I'm never particularly worried about the fact that most prophecies I listen to will be a mixture of God's words and people's words: there is always so much joy and adventure in processing everything with the Holy Spirit. He has promised to lead us into all truth, so let's not get hung up about the fact that most of us have very large 'L-plates' on.

The New Testament is very clear that revelation has to be weighed;

prophecies have to be tested to see if they are from God:

> *Two or three prophets should speak, and the others should weigh carefully what is said.*
> 1 Corinthians 14:29

> *Do not treat prophecies with contempt but test them all; hold on to what is good.*
> 1 Thessalonians 5:20-21

> *Dear friends, do not believe every spirit, but test the spirits to see whether they are from God, because many false prophets have gone out into the world.*
> 1 John 4:1

So the Bible is fairly clear – weighing prophecy is important. It's not always easy, though:

- We need to have **faith** and believe Jesus' promise in John 10 that his sheep will be able to identify his voice and not follow after a stranger. That's what he promises. And he also promises us in John 16 that the Holy Spirit will lead us into all truth. The Spirit of Truth is dwelling within us and it's through him that we recognise the true voice of our Good Shepherd.

- We need to be growing in the gift of **discernment** – one of the most valuable gifts in any church. It's a spiritual gift that we can, and should, be eagerly desiring and praying for. It's a vital gift to have when we are testing revelation.

- It's also important to clarify that when we weigh or judge a prophecy we are deciding if it is from God or not; we are **not judging the person** or questioning their spirituality. We all need to be open to having our own prophecies weighed, but when we are weighing other people's prophecies we need to be clear that we are not making judgements about that person, we are simply testing the prophecy.

So an important starting point in weighing prophecy is to test all revelation with a good measure of faith, with discernment, and grace.

In the previous chapter we began to look at the characteristics of God's voice. What we're going to do now is examine what should be our main guidelines for weighing revelation.

1. Where has it comes from?

A fundamental question to ask is: what is the spirit behind the prophecy? Revelation can come from different sources:

- the Holy Spirit,
- our own thoughts, motives and agendas i.e. our souls, or
- the influence of an evil spirit

A counterfeit word – a word definitely not from God – may actually pass many of the following tests, but we may first need to discern the spirit behind it.

There is an interesting example of this in Acts 16:16-18:

> *Once when we were going to the place of prayer, we were met by a female slave who had a spirit by which she predicted the future. She earned a great deal of money for her owners by fortune-telling. She followed Paul and the rest of us, shouting, "These men are servants of the Most High God, who are telling you the way to be saved." She kept this up for many days. Finally Paul became so annoyed that he turned round and said to the spirit, "In the name of Jesus Christ I command you to come out of her!" At that moment the spirit left her.*

The girl's words were 100% accurate but it was an evil spirit speaking through her. Paul discerned the spirit behind what she was saying.

If you ever feel uneasy when you are listening to a prophecy – if your spirit is troubled and you have real lack of peace about it – this could be a sign that the source of the prophecy is not God. And whenever you are weighing a prophecy start off by asking the Holy Spirit whether it is his words you are hearing. Get in the habit of asking the Holy Spirit, *"Is this you…?"*

2. Does it line up with scripture?

All true revelation from the Holy Spirit is going to echo with biblical truth. So when we are testing prophecies we need to be asking whether or not they line up with the Bible's words, concepts and attitudes.

So, for example, the Bible teaches us that God is love (1 John 4:8) and therefore accurate prophecy will be in alignment with God's nature of love. True prophecy will always be consistent with what the Bible teaches us about God. It will reveal him and his nature in the same way that the Bible reveals him.

True prophecy does not conflict with scripture – though it may conflict with our personal understanding and interpretation of scripture! Or our doctrinal stance. This is one of the reasons why prophetic ministry has to be rooted in community. It's only when we are processing prophecy with others that we will get the broad and balanced perspective on our own interpretation of the Bible that will help us weigh prophetic words.

The more we fill ourselves with the Word – the Bible – the more we will be able to know and discern the voice of God, and thus weigh prophecy accurately.

3.   Does it strengthen, encourage and comfort?

1 Corinthians 14:3 is one of those verses that everyone operating in the prophetic should know by heart:

> *But the one who prophesies speaks to people for their strengthening, encouraging and comfort.*

This verse gives us such a good test of prophecy, and it's worth having a closer look at the three key words it contains:

- **Strengthening** (or 'edification' in some English translations)

  The Greek word is *oikodome* and literally means to build a home (*oikos* 'a home', *demo* 'to build'). It's a building word, and carries with it the sense of establishing and improving; to build up where others have torn down; the promotion of spiritual growth. So good questions to ask when weighing a prophecy are:

Does this prophecy lead me to have a stronger relationship with God? Is it building up my relationship with God?

- **Encouragement** (or 'exhortation' in some English translations)

  The Greek word is *paraklesis* and literally means 'a calling or summoning near.' (It's worth noting that this word comes from the same root word as *parakletos* which is Jesus' name for the Holy Spirit in John 14, 15 and 16.) This word conveys the sense of being cheered on and called into a better place. So again, a good question to ask is:

  Is this prophecy cheering me on and leading me into a better place in my walk with God?

- **Comfort**

  The Greek word is *paramythia* and the literal translation is 'close speech' (*para* 'near', *muthos* 'speech'). It describes coming really close to someone and speaking gently to them: a picture of God whispering a tender message of comfort to his friends, God getting so close that he's whispering in your ear.

So you can see how these three words give us a useful framework for weighing prophecy.

Now a perfectly valid question to ask at this point is:

What about corrective words? Words of discipline? Where do they fit in?

These are valid questions, but the end result and final purpose of any prophecy – even quite a heavy, corrective one – has got to be strengthening, encouragement and comfort. If God needs to speak discipline into our lives, he doesn't just leave us in a place of conviction – he leads from that place into a place of grace and freedom.

If a prophecy doesn't ultimately strengthen, encourage or comfort – if the effect of a prophecy is discouragement or condemnation – then it shouldn't be accepted. If someone prophesies over you and you're left feeling discouraged or really confused or condemned you do not have to receive it.

4. Does it point people to Jesus and bring him glory and honour?

In John 16:14 when Jesus is describing the revelatory ministry of the Spirit he speaks these words:

> *He will glorify me because it is from me that he will receive what he will make known to you.*

When the Holy Spirit brings us revelation, whether it's a dream, vision or word, Jesus is going to be glorified. If a prophecy is in any way magnifying a person or ministry, such that our eyes are taken off Jesus, then it's probably not of God.

So some good questions to ask are:

Is this prophecy moving me closer to Jesus? Or is it leading me somewhere else, or to someone else?

Is this prophecy leading me to love Jesus more, or does it lead me away from my single-hearted devotion to him?

5. Does it resonate? Does it bring a sense of peace?

This is probably the most subjective of these tests, but it is an important one. Prophecy is spiritual, not logical, and we need to learn to listen to the response of our spirits whenever we hear a prophecy being given. As we grow in relationship with the Holy Spirit we will grow in sensitivity to his workings, and we will be able to know when a prophecy resonates. It's that inner, convicting witness of the Holy Spirit – which is very hard to teach people. It really is a case of 'you know it when you know it'! We certainly need the Holy Spirit in order to weigh prophecy:

> *The Spirit searches all things, even the deep things of God*
> 1 Corinthians 2:10

The more we are filled with, and moving in, the power of the Holy Spirit, the easier we will find it to weigh prophecy.

So, they are the main tests for weighing prophecy. There are however a few further things to consider:

- Is the prophecy given in love? A lack of love probably indicates an unhealthy prophetic ministry and someone ministering from wrong motives. The prophecy may not be wrong, but it's a good question to ask. If you perceive that it wasn't given in love then the bar for 'passing' the prophecy has to be a lot higher.

- Nobody should be exempt from the judging and weighing process. There's always a temptation to skip the weighing and judging if the prophecy is from a 'big name' or someone in a leadership position. As we grow a prophetic culture in our churches we need to be very clear with people that everyone expects their prophecies to be weighed.

- It's OK to seek confirmation. If God seems to be saying something new or radical to you, then you can ask him for confirmation. Take your prophecies to spiritually mature, trusted people and if they do not confirm the words you have received from the Lord, a few alarm bells should go off.

- Does it come to pass? When prophecies are given about future events there will be a delay until we can ask this most obvious question, but it's important to note the accuracy of predictive prophecy, so that we can both learn from mistakes and be encouraged when we get it right.

Responding to Revelation

Once we are confident that we are dealing with God-given revelation, we can then move on to the absolutely key issue of how we respond to God's words to us – what do we do when God speaks into our lives?

When God speaks to us he speaks for a purpose and he looks for a response. There is a profound intentionality to God's spoken words to us; we have to beware a casual attitude to them. We need to be **active responders** rather than passive receivers. It's all too easy to gratefully receive a prophecy, enjoy the momentary 'buzz' that comes with being prophesied over, and then have pretty much forgotten it by tea-time.

When God speaks into our lives he wants us to work with him to fulfil the true potential of his word to us, to produce something beautiful and long lasting. We need to be cautious of the, *"Well, if it's God it'll happen"* mentality, especially if the word is something to do with God's call on our life. Prophecies are amazing offers from God, but are not absolutes, and we need to consider our responsibility to respond in faith to his word to us.

We also need to ensure that any pride or arrogance in our hearts will not get in the way of us clearly hearing and responding to whatever it is that God is saying to us. To receive a prophecy, and actively respond to it, we must have a humble and open heart, so that we choose God's agenda above any of our own agendas, and are prepared to let his word refine us as necessary.

Using the Learning Circle

The Learning Circle is a fantastic tool for processing revelation and takes us back to the biblical principle of 'hear and obey':

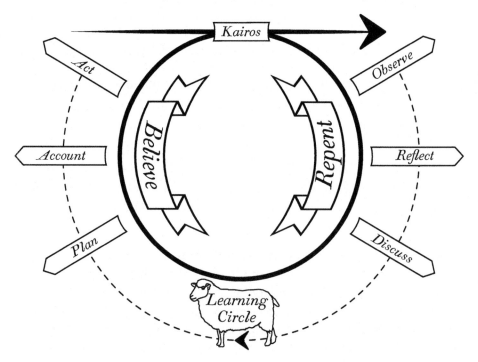

The Learning Circle is one of the fundamental tools of discipleship developed within 3DM[9]. It is based on the words of Jesus at the beginning of Mark's gospel and at the end of the Sermon on the Mount.

> *After John was put in prison, Jesus went into Galilee, proclaiming the good news of God. "The time has come", he said. "The kingdom of God has come near. **Repent and believe** the good news!"*
> Mark 1:14-15

> *"Therefore everyone who **hears** these words of mine and **puts them into practice** is like a wise man who built his house on the rock"*
> Matthew 7:24

The Learning Circle is designed to help us ask ourselves the two fundamental questions of Christian discipleship:

What is God saying to me?

What am I going to do about it?

If we take the general principles of the Learning Circle, it gives us an incredibly useful framework for turning prophetic revelation into something tangible, grounded and real. It gives us a framework for how to respond when God speaks into our lives.

The Learning Circle starts with *kairos* which is the Greek word for 'time' in Mark 1:15. This is not chronological, sequential time (the Greek word for that is *chronos*); rather a significant moment when something notable happens. *Kairos* time is when God breaks into our reality and really gets our attention. A *kairos* moment occurs every time we hear him speak to us.

When God speaks – when we recognise a *kairos* – we need to see it as an opportunity for growth, an opportunity to become more like Jesus. In fact a great question to ask about revelation is:

How can I respond to this prophecy so that I can become more like

---

[9] For more information about it please have a look at *Building a Discipling Culture* (Pawleys Island: 3DM Publishing, 2014) by Mike Breen.

Jesus?

The Learning Circle helps us both process what God is saying to us and then respond in a way that enables us to grow in our discipleship. The two key words, which define the process, are **repent** and **believe**.

- 'Repent' is about changing the way we think (observe, reflect and then discuss what God is saying to us) and is usually an **internal** process.

- 'Believe' is about stepping out in faith (we plan our response, we are accountable about what we are going to do, and then we act on the word God has given us) and is an **external** process.

So this is a great reminder that when God speaks into our lives there needs to be both an internal and external response.

The Learning Circle leads us to ask two questions in response to prophecy:

1. *What internal change needs to take place in me in order for this word to become reality?*

2. *What step of faith do I need to take – what change do I need to make to my life – to see this word become reality?*

If we ask ourselves these two questions every time we receive a prophecy, and are accountable with the answers, we will become active responders to the prophetic, and God's divine purposes as he speaks to us will be fully realised. The Learning Circle reminds us of the transformative power of God's living word to us – the prophetic should both change the way we think and change the way we behave/act. The simplest prophetic word has transformative power.

The Circle and Prophetic People

The Learning Circle is a fantastic way to process prophetic revelation – when God is speaking to us about our own lives. But it also highlights two potential dangers for prophetic people:

1. Prophetic people can have lots of personal revelation, but the

danger is they don't have the discipline of the rest of the Circle – they do 'Observe' and 'Reflect', but then stop. This is often true for more introverted people. They hear God easily, and know what God is saying about their lives; but because they stop at 'Reflect' they are passive, not active, responders and don't engage fully with the process of transformation.

It's good to recognise that for many prophetic people there is a real cost to externalising revelation and sharing their prophetic words with other people. We can feel vulnerable as we attempt to explain the things God has been showing us and expose precious revelation to the scrutiny of others. The temptation can be to be either apologetic and play it down (*"Well it's probably not God but I did get this vague sense that he is saying this to me…"*) or to be defensive and directive (*"This is the word of the Lord to me and you'd better take it very seriously…"*). This is why it's so important to create a church culture where it's normal and accepted to ask each other the question, *"What is God saying to you?"* and people are used to talking about all the wonderful and challenging things God is revealing to them.

If we never externalise revelation it can become stagnant as we dwell and dwell on it. There is the danger of thinking that everything we think we hear from God is right. Whereas moving it around the Learning Circle allows it to become shaped and sharpened by others. It's not good enough simply to hear God's voice – we have to allow ourselves to be refined and shaped by God's voice – and the Learning Circle reminds us the maximum potential for the effectiveness of God's word is when we involve others.

2. The other danger that the Learning Circle highlights is that of going straight from the *kairos* to 'Act'. Someone hears from God and then acts on the revelation without taking it properly round the Circle. For some of us this represents a huge temptation because we want to go it alone and do it all by ourselves: involving others will surely slow us down. God's said it so it must be right. But this attitude actually reveals a root of pride and self-reliance that ends up crippling prophetic people. We would be so much more effective if we brought other people into the process, properly discussing our revelation with others

and then being held accountable for whatever we feel God is calling us to do.

With both these potential dangers the Learning Circle highlights the fact that responding to prophecy should take place in some kind of context of community. It gives the prophetic person a systematic process so that he or she is able to share, put into practice and live out what God says. It helps the prophetic word be made flesh and helps make things more grounded.

Using the lens of Revelation, Interpretation, Application

This is another very useful tool for processing prophecy. It's easy to understand and teach, and once people grasp it, it prevents many problems.

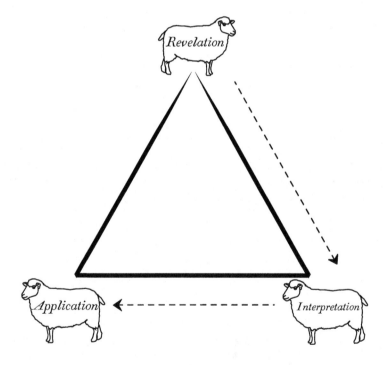

There are three parts to any prophecy:

- **Revelation**: the 'raw data'; the picture, word, dream given to the person by God. Going back to the Learning Circle, this would be the *kairos* and 'Observe' (with perhaps a little bit of

'Reflect').

- **Interpretation**: what the revelation means. This would be 'Reflect' and 'Discuss' in the Learning Circle.

- **Application**: this is the answer to the question: *"What am I going to do about it?"* and relates to the 'Plan', 'Account', 'Act' part of the Learning Circle.

All three parts are equally important, and a mature prophetic culture is one where emphasis and training is applied to all three.

In the same way that the Learning Circle is so useful in ensuring that we are active responders to prophecy, rather than passive receivers, using the lens of 'Revelation, Interpretation, Application' helps to ensure that the whole prophetic process is properly administered. To be mature practitioners of prophecy we need to take hold of each of the three parts separately.

The hard reality is that most prophetic people are great at revelation, all right at interpretation, and really poor at application. If we expect one person to deliver all three parts of a prophecy we are going to run into difficulties. And most problems or controversy associated with prophetic ministry are actually not because of weak revelation, but because the other two were wrong.

It is all too easy to attach our own interpretations to revelation we have received. Faulty interpretation can be a major problem, so we need to proceed with caution. We should always ask the Lord for an interpretation to revelation he gives us, but be content to simply speak out an un-interpreted revelation if that is all we have. Often God will give the interpretation to someone else.

When it comes to the application of prophecy, this is best discerned within a context of community and with people who are gifted in strategy. In fact in my experience it is usually apostles who are best at application – this is another reason why prophets need to be friends with apostles!

Believe and Pray

> As the rain and the snow come down from heaven, and
> do not return to it without watering the earth and making

it bud and flourish, so that it yields seed for the sower and bread for the eater, so is my word that goes out from my mouth: It will not return to me empty, but will accomplish what I desire and achieve the purpose for which I sent it.

In these verses from Isaiah 55 we see the power of God's spoken word. If we hear, weigh and actively respond to the prophecies he gives us, then we can expect to see them fulfilled in our lives and in our churches. What may seem like impossible promises from a human perspective can turn into living reality as we choose to align ourselves with his word to us and commit to praying. Our God has unlimited resources and nothing is impossible for him.

Prayer is a vital component of responding to prophecy. We can pray in faith that his word will be fulfilled, confident that it will accomplish his purposes. The enemy of the sheep will always conspire to oppose the promises of God to us, but we have the authority to lay hold of what God has said and bind the devil (Matthew 16:19). If you have prophetic promises that you are longing to see fulfilled I would really encourage you to keep bringing them before the Lord and intercede for them. Have confidence in his spoken word to you!

Part Four

The Bottom Line

Chapter 11

Covenant

If we're going to create a culture where disciples can hear the voice of the Good Shepherd, where prophetic people can flourish, and where church communities are listening communities that fully embrace the call of God, then we need to have good foundations in place. Over the years I've come to see that the most important of these foundations is a thorough understanding of the two fundamental themes that wind their way through the whole of scripture: *'covenant'* and *'kingdom'*.

These two themes give us an approach to understanding the entire biblical narrative: they are like the double helix of spiritual DNA in the Bible. The great truths of *'covenant'* – relationship with God – and *'kingdom'* – the responsibility to represent God – lead us all the way through scripture.

And not only does an understanding of these themes anchor the prophetic, it also provides a biblical perspective that covers the whole spectrum of prophetic experience. Applying the paradigm of 'covenant and kingdom' to absolutely everything we do and say in the prophetic is going to ensure our ministry is grounded, biblical and healthy. It's the bottom line.[10]

So in this chapter we're going to look in some depth at the concept of 'covenant' and how it must shape our whole approach to prophecy. And in the next chapter we'll examine 'kingdom'.

....

[10] For a more in-depth study see *Covenant and Kingdom* (Pawleys Island: 3DM Publishing, 2011) by Mike Breen

The Theology of Covenant: Relationship with God

In the secular sense of the word a covenant is a binding agreement or legal contract that two or more parties have with each other. But the biblical perspective on covenant is much richer and more profound, and encapsulates what it means to be in a committed relationship with someone. The theology of covenant is about the committed and steadfast relationship between God and his people.

Relationship with God is of course one of the overarching themes of scripture, and using the word 'covenant' to summarize this is very useful as we seek to grasp the big picture of what the Bible is all about. The theme of covenant is woven throughout the whole biblical narrative as God calls people into relationship with him, and then out of that relationship gives them a new identity. Right at the start of the Bible the Genesis story carries with it the profound truth that we are created in the likeness of God: right at the beginning our identity is defined by our Creator and tied to his. In the lives of Abraham, Moses and David we see God taking the initiative in establishing a covenantal relationship with them. But of course the tragedy of the Old Testament story is that time after time the majority of people rejected the opportunity to be in a committed and loving relationship with their God.

When we look at the life of Jesus we get a clearer insight into the theme of covenant as we see him revealing the depth of relationship he enjoyed with his heavenly Father, and then inviting his own followers into a covenantal relationship with himself. Through the Cross the Son of God offers every single person the opportunity to be reconnected to the Father in the 'oneness' that was there at creation: the perfect union of creator and created. As Christians we are called into an incredible relationship with the Father: a deep, radical and intimate covenant with the God of heaven.

We can understand the impact of the covenant relationship that we have with God through three essential elements: Father, Identity and Obedience. These words help us calibrate and guard the very basis of our understanding about hearing the voice of God.

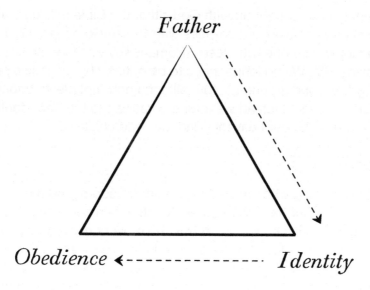

Father

Obedience ← ------------- *Identity*

- Father

Our perfect heavenly Father calls us into a covenantal relationship with himself. We know God as Father: Jesus revealed his relationship with his heavenly Father and he invites us into that same relationship.

We live our lives in the knowledge that the most loving, kind and generous person we will ever meet is extending his arms to us and constantly watching over us. In this relationship we experience amazing love, acceptance and forgiveness; all of our needs for affirmation and approval are met; we know that God is pleased with us. We are fully known and fully loved as the Father lavishes his unending compassion and mercy upon us.

- Identity

Out of this amazing sense of security we discover a new family identity as his children. Our identity flows from our heavenly Father. We are created in his likeness; he gives us our identity; we are one with Christ.

Our sense of value, security and confidence come from outside ourselves as God tells us that we are his children. We bear his name and everything he has is ours.

Our identity is so caught up with God's that the Bible tells us that we are heirs of heaven and co-heirs with Christ (Romans 8:17, Titus 3:7). In fact we are one with Jesus (Romans 6:5-8, 1 Corinthians 1:30, Colossians 3:3). We no longer have to be defined by the labels placed on us by the world around us: too tall, too short, not clever enough, not sporty enough. Instead we attune ourselves to the new identity spoken over us by our heavenly Dad: beloved children.

• Obedience

It's out of knowing who we are that we find freedom, and the desire, to obey our heavenly Father. We obey him because this is a true reflection of who we are; this is the most consistent way of expressing our identity. When we know in the very depths of our being that we're God's beloved children, our desire to do all that our Father wants us to do will flow naturally from this place of identity.

Obedience is not the starting point for relationship with God. If obedience doesn't come out of identity then it comes out of legalism and striving, when we try to earn God's favour. If we don't accept our given identity as children of God who are loved unconditionally, we try to find our spiritual identity through obedience. Then we fall into the trap of living by law – the error the Pharisees made. And trying to live by law is a discouraging pathway that always ends in failure and guilt.

Because we are God's children he is already pleased with us! So we are free from legalistic observance and we instead live under grace. Obedience is always an act of love: because of our shared covenant identity with Jesus, we do the things he did. All of our dreams and ambitions for what we can achieve through life are fulfilled in our simple obedience to God's word.

Rooting the Prophetic in Covenant

Firstly, let's remind ourselves that part of the fundamental role of prophecy is to reveal the nature of God: to demonstrate what he's really like. So, as we saw in Chapter 8, true prophecy reveals the Father and represents his incredible heart of love and compassion. When we prophesy over people we have the opportunity to represent our Father to them, to give them a glimpse of the One who is infinitely good and kind. His spoken word is going to be representative of his nature, and this has implications for both the manner in which we prophesy and the words we use to communicate the prophecy. Both have to be aligned with the true nature of our heavenly Father who calls us into covenantal relationship with himself.

As prophetic people we have the privilege of ministering out of a revelation of the Father. Prophecy starts with understanding what he is like. We proclaim him, we represent him, and we root ourselves in all that he is. If we don't have a covenantal understanding of who our perfect heavenly Father is, if we think he is judgemental or critical, if we project our broken and worldly image of fatherhood onto God, then that will adversely affect our prophetic ministry. But if we know God as abundantly good, kind and loving, then our ministry can flow from this place. We shouldn't be surprised that the New Testament perspective on prophecy is focused on encouraging, strengthening and comforting people, because, from a covenantal point of view, that is absolutely God's heart for us. Mature prophetic ministry speaks the Father's heart and this should be reflected in the texture of any prophetic word we give.

A covenant mindset releases all of us into the joy of hearing God's voice because the bottom line is that **hearing God is about who you are, not what you do**. We cannot earn the right to hear his voice; it's not something we achieve through hard work or 'super-spirituality'. Hearing God flows out of relationship, pure and simple. It's about **being** before doing. Knowing our true identity as children of God releases us into hearing his voice – because fathers like speaking to their children. In fact a deep understanding of this covenant relationship takes us to a place where prophecy becomes less and less an activity that we **do**; rather it becomes a beautiful reflection and overflow of who we **are**.

As we journey deeper into the riches of our covenant with God we find the antidote for legalism and striving. We can't strive to hear our Father's voice. The truth of covenant reminds us that we simply align and attune our hearts with his; being still and knowing that he is God. As we focus on his glory and majesty we can rest in that place of perfect love and enjoy the fact that we are his children. The more we are rooted in our covenant relationship with God the more we can expect to see and hear prophetically because our perspective will be increasingly aligned with his.

Without an understanding of covenant we will be tempted to behave as spiritual orphans rather than beloved children. We will try to earn God's favour – try to earn his gifts and anointing. We will compare ourselves with others and the level of anointing they seem to have. We will strive for success.

The Battle for Identity

We need to recognise the nature of the battle we are in, because the enemy will always attack us on identity. When Jesus encountered Satan in the desert it was Jesus' identity as God's son that was targeted:

"If you are the Son of God...."

As Jesus' representatives we face the same temptations. Insecurity and brokenness around our identity has the potential to completely de-rail our prophetic ministry. The way of the world – competition, ambition, striving, appetite, self-righteousness and success – has affected many in the church and these are destructive forces as far as the prophetic is concerned. There is a real danger of finding our identity in our ministry rather than in God.

When we haven't had a deep revelation of our covenant identity, and lack security in who we really are, then we become vulnerable to three fundamental fears that all have their roots in identity issues:

- Fear of **rejection**

  I have to strive for approval and acceptance. I need to prophesy in a way that will please people.

- Fear of **lack**

  God's voice is a scarce resource. I'm afraid I won't hear anything. If I make a mistake there will be no more anointing.

- Fear of **failure**

  I need to succeed in prophetic ministry. Others need to see me as a success. It will be terrible if I get it wrong.

Insecurity and prophecy are not a good mix. However, the more we root ourselves in the reality of our covenantal relationship with God and take on a mindset of 'beloved child' rather than 'orphan', the less susceptible we will be to these fears. A covenant mentality gives us confidence and security; being secure in our identity and having confidence in who God is. We can be secure because God has given us our new identity – of oneness with himself. Security is essential for operating in prophetic ministry – being absolutely secure in our identity and in the nature of our heavenly Father.

As his children we have access to all his resources. He is abundantly kind and generous and will pour his prophetic gifts upon us if we ask him. He delights to use his beloved children to carry his words of hope and assurance to people who need to hear them. A covenant perspective tells us that there is enough for everyone in our Father's family, and so we can live and prophesy out of the kindness and generosity of God. We live generously and we give away what we've got, because we know there is always more.

When we really have a covenant mindset it changes our approach to ministry. The truth of covenant strips away pride and reputation, competitiveness and striving for success, and takes us to a place where all that matters is God's reputation and glory. In this place we enter into the rest of just being children of God and take joy in the fact that our ministry is basically that of representing our Father. We simply get to join in with whatever he is doing. As John Wimber used to say, *"I'm just change in his pocket; he can spend me however he chooses."*[11]

Coming back to those three fundamental fears we can see how the Father's perfect love drives them away:

- A mindset of the Father's ***approval*** declares:

  My heavenly Father loves me and it is from him that I receive everlasting approval. I'm free to prophesy as the Spirit leads; I don't have to seek approval from others.

- A mindset of the Father's ***abundance*** declares:

---

[11] Carol Wimber - *John Wimber: The Way it Was* (Hodder & Stoughton, 1999)

God is good and he is generous with his gifts; there is so much to go around, we can all join in. I can give prophecies freely and generously.

- A mindset of the Father's **acceptance** declares:

  I find fulfilment in simple obedience. My ambition is to only say what I hear the Father saying.

The truth of our covenant with God secures and guards prophecy because it keeps drawing us back to the truth that it is only out of relationship with God that we can learn to hear his voice, and as we step out and prophesy over people we do that from a place of rest, assurance and affirmation.

And a covenantal perspective helps us to respond well to prophecy. Whenever God speaks to us there is an invitation to grow closer in relationship with him. When we receive a prophecy, we should not simply see it as a set of instructions to be followed, but respond to it as coming from the Father's heart and hear the heart and the substance behind it.

Pursuing the Presence

Many people want to know how they can grow in prophecy; how they can move powerfully in prophetic anointing and become much sharper and accurate in the prophecies they deliver.

Ultimately, we will grow in prophecy to the extent that we spend time in God's presence. We can read a hundred books on prophecy, and visit many prophetic conferences, but unless we are growing in covenantal fellowship with God it will pretty much remain theory. Prophecy is all about relationship; it's not what you know, but **whom** you know.

In 1 Samuel 3 we find the story of the boy Samuel who would grow up to become one of the greatest prophets of the Old Testament. We are told that in *In those days the word of the Lord was rare; there were not many visions.* But God spoke to the young boy as he was lying in an unexpected and significant place: in the temple by the Ark of Covenant. The Ark was symbolic of the manifest presence and glory of the Lord; the focal point of God dwelling amongst, and speaking to, his people:

> *"There, above the cover between the two cherubim that are over the ark, I will meet with you and give you all my commands for the Israelites."*
> Exodus 25:22

The story of the young Samuel provides a powerful picture for us: it was as he rested before the Ark in God's presence that Samuel heard God's voice, in a time when the word of the Lord was scarce.

It's a fairly obvious point to make, but if we want to grow in the prophetic we've got to spend time with God. As we journey deeper into the wonders of this covenant relationship we need to be people who will lay aside many pressing demands on our time so that we can find our own resting place in God's presence and learn to hear his voice, just like Samuel. The closer we are to him, the easier it will be to hear him. Prophecy is basically relational; it's simply spending time in God's presence and learning to hear his voice.

In the Psalms we see how David was someone who pursued the presence of God:

> *One thing I ask from the Lord, this only do I seek: that I may dwell in the house of the Lord all the days of my life, to gaze on the beauty of the Lord and to seek him in his temple.*
> Psalm 27:4

> *How lovely is your dwelling place, O Lord Almighty! My soul yearns, even faints, for the courts of the Lord; my heart and my flesh cry out for the living God... Better is one day in your courts than a thousand elsewhere; I would rather be a doorkeeper in the house of my God than dwell in the tents of the wicked.*
> Psalm 84:1-2,10

David learnt to prioritise the presence of God. In a world full of distractions, pressures and busyness, we too need to maintain in our hearts a clear vision of fellowship with God and prioritise an abiding connection with our heavenly Father.

So how can we do this, this greatest of all pursuits?

- We first of all receive encouragement from the fact that God initiates relationship with us. He desires deep relationship with us even more than we do. As John writes in his first letter, *We love him because he first loved us* (1 John 4:19).

- Fellowship with the Lord requires a determination to pursue God daily, so we need to make sure we have regular times that we set aside for enjoying his presence. We will meet him through the spiritual disciplines of prayer, worship and reading the Bible.

- But as well as regular devotional time there is also the **lifestyle** of knowing and acknowledging his presence all the time, even in the busyness of everyday life. This is about learning how to connect with him wherever you are and whatever you are doing, whether you are in a meeting at work or in the supermarket. It's about being God-conscious; seeking out his manifest presence all the time. A couple of things that have really helped me are:

  » regularly taking time throughout my day to stop and thank God that he's with me. It's very simple but very effective

  » playing worship music whenever I'm in the car and using this to engage with his presence

- It's important to find out what works for you, because different things work for different people. What do you do that makes you feel most connected to God? Once you've got hold of these keys, then build them into your life.

- When you are feeling tired or low, make the decision to let God satisfy you, rather than worldly things. It's a great discipline to allow his loving and fiery presence to refresh and restore us, rather than food or alcohol or other worldly comforts.

- There is sometimes a battle to encounter God's presence. In the Bible people often met with God in the desert, but the desert also was symbolic of the place where the demonic dwelt. We have to be aware that the enemy will do all he can to stop us spending time in God's presence, to limit our intimacy with God. His tactic is to distract us and discourage us. But if we are forewarned we can be forearmed.

We can find inspiration from people like Brother Lawrence, a seventeenth-century French monk, who learned to practice the presence of God at all times, even doing the most mundane tasks:

> *"There is not in the world a kind of life more sweet and delightful, than that of a continual conversation with God; those only can comprehend it who practice and experience it."*

> *"The time of busyness does not with me differ from the time of prayer; and in the noise and clatter of my kitchen, while several persons are at the same time calling for different things, I possess God in as great tranquillity as if I were upon my knees at the blessed sacrament."*[12]

Covenant-focused Ministry

As we grow and develop as prophetic people, we should eagerly desire to minister to people in ways that establish and strengthen them in their covenant identity as much loved children of a perfect heavenly Father. Prophecy is a fantastic resource in any Christian community for taking people deeper into relationship with God.

We can partner with the Holy Spirit to prophesy thus:

- revealing the Father's love – sharing God's heart with people so that they are drawn closer into relationship with him

- speaking words of identity that reveal how the Father sees each of us and the unique ways he has created us

- encouraging people to follow Jesus more closely and become more like him, strengthening them in Christ-like character

- calling people to obedience and covenantal faithfulness

Covenant is about 'oneness' and the covenantal role of prophecy is to draw people closer to the Father and to facilitate the journey of becoming more like him. As we draw closer to him, our hearts will be more aligned to his, and what we speak prophetically will in turn cause others to become closer to him.

---

[12] Brother Lawrence - *The Practice of The Presence of God*

The great thing about understanding the themes of 'covenant' and 'kingdom' is that we need the balance of both. And as we see in the next chapter, God doesn't just call us into his fiery presence, but he sends us out from that place. The more we grow in relationship with him, the more he invites us to **step out** with him.

Chapter 12

Kingdom

We've seen how the covenantal theme of God pursuing relationship with humanity is central to the whole biblical narrative: as we take hold of this truth we encounter the majestic love of our heavenly Father and are affirmed in our identity as his children. But there is another essential theme that makes up the fabric of scripture, and the weft to the warp of 'covenant' is the concept of 'kingdom' – a word that we use to encapsulate the idea that as God's covenant people we are given **responsibility**.

At its heart, the theme of 'kingdom' is about the responsibility to represent God, to extend his kingship – his rule – and to manifest the kingdom of God on earth.

When we consider the practical outworking of a kingdom perspective it's vital that we are first and foremost grounded in a covenant mindset. Without this mindset we become driven, legalistic and task-focused, all of which is toxic, both in our walk as disciples and to our prophetic ministry. But unless we actively take hold of the theology of 'kingdom' and live in both paradigms we will see little breakthrough in the world around us and will be a people of unfulfilled potential.

The Great Commandment (*"Love!"*) goes hand-in-hand with the Great Commission (*"Go!"*). The essence of what Jesus says to us is:

"Come to me, and then go out into all the world."

Kingdom Theology: Responsibility as Representatives

The biblical concept of 'kingdom' is about the responsibility God gives to those with whom he has established a covenant. It is about representing the King and taking the responsibility to act on his behalf and extend his kingdom here on earth.

If 'covenant' is about **being**, then 'kingdom' is about **doing**: relationship **and** responsibility.

In the creation story, not only did God make us in his own image but he also intended that we would represent him. People were designed and destined to be God's representatives, to steward, oversee and care for all creation, and to do this in dependency on him. That is the original commission.

> *"Be fruitful and increase in number; fill the earth and subdue it."*
> Genesis 1:28

'Kingdom' always follows 'covenant', because responsibility always follows relationship. So God's commission to mankind followed on from the covenantal act of creating us in his likeness and defining our identity through his. Our fundamental responsibility as human beings is to represent God on the earth.

In studying the life of Moses we can see a great illustration of God establishing the foundational truths of both covenant and kingdom in someone's life, weaving together the threads of relationship and responsibility. Moses couldn't walk in authority and power, as God's representative, until his identity was settled. When God first called him, his reaction revealed an identity focussed on insecurity, failure and fear. So God's response was to call him close, to reveal to Moses more of his divine character, and to promise that he'd be with him constantly. But alongside this covenantal invitation there was a call to embrace his destiny – to take hold of the authority God gave him to lead the people, and to defeat the powers that held the people in captivity.

The theme of kingdom finds its greatest expression in Jesus Christ. The King of heaven took on flesh and chose to walk on this earth as the perfect representation of God's kingly authority and power. The reality and substance of heaven – forgiveness, healing, deliverance, freedom – became available through Jesus. He was the perfect conduit of God's kingdom on earth. He brought the full revelation of the kingdom: if we want to know what God's kingdom looks like we simply have to look at the ministry of Jesus.

At Nazareth he declared the manifesto of the kingdom he had come to bring:

> "The Spirit of the Lord is on me, because he has anointed me to proclaim good news to the poor. He has sent me to proclaim freedom for the prisoners and recovery of sight for the blind, to to set the oppressed free, to proclaim the year of the Lord's favour."
> Luke 4:18-19

In his earthly ministry the Son of Man was the perfect representation and channel of this kingdom. It was manifested as he healed the sick, cast out demons, forgave sinners and cleansed lepers. Through his sacrificial death on the cross he brought the ultimate victory of the kingdom over our ancient enemies: he destroyed the power of sin, sickness and death. He also restored humanity's role to rule on behalf of God with this commission:

> "All authority in heaven and on earth has been given to me. Therefore go..."
> Matthew 28:18-19

Jesus taught his first disciples to represent him by living as he lived, doing as he did and loving as he loved. He taught them to reveal the kingdom of God, sending them out to do all that they had seen him do. So they went out and demonstrated the reality of the kingdom by healing the sick, delivering the oppressed and declaring the good news:

> He gave them power and authority to drive out all demons and to cure diseases, and he sent them out to proclaim the kingdom of God and to heal those who were ill.
> Luke 9:1-2

As disciples of Jesus we, too, carry his authority to establish his rule and reign wherever we go, in order to extend his kingdom and rescue people from darkness. The kingdom is about the King's domain, and the more familiar we get with his domain, the more confidence we have to operate within it. As we get to know the nature of his rule, we can speak out aspects of the kingdom with confidence and authority.

The reality of the new covenant means we are one with him, so **his manifesto is our manifesto**. Our responsibility as disciples is to represent the fullness of the kingdom of God to the world around us. Our responsibility is to advance his kingdom – to actively challenge and push back the reign of darkness – knowing that all the resources of heaven are available to us.

Jesus taught us to pray, "*Your kingdom come, your will be done on earth as in heaven*" (Matthew 6:10). We are to pray kingdom prayers – that the reality of heaven is released on the earth. When we pray we ask God to bring his world into ours: his world where there is no sin, sadness, or sickness. Because these things do not exist in heaven we have the authority to pray that they will diminish in our communities here on earth.

We are called to *Seek first the kingdom of God and his righteousness* (Matthew 6:33), which means that we seek to see the Lordship of Jesus – the King's domain – in all circumstances of life. Disease is met by healing, sin is met by forgiveness, and oppression is met by liberty as the kingdom advances.

A Summary of Kingdom

In the same way that the central truths of 'covenant' can be conveyed through three essential elements, a simple way to understand the 'kingdom' perspective is by using three key words: King, Authority and Power.

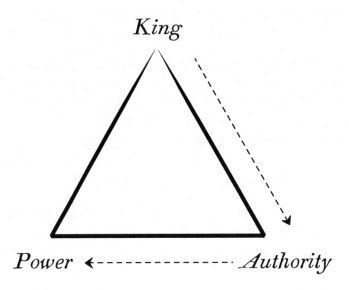

- King

The God that we love and worship is the King of the universe, creator and sustainer of everything, the majestic ruler of heaven and earth. And he seeks to extend his loving rule through the lives of all people. As disciples of Jesus, we need to have this incredible King as Lord of every area of our lives.

- Authority

Authority simply means the qualification to act. As we choose to carry the responsibility of representing the King, he gives us his authority. This authority gives us the freedom to act on the King's behalf. But, as 'kingdom' always follows on from 'covenant', our authority needs to be based on our secure identity of being one with Christ.

- Power

Our God is the all-powerful King. The Bible leaves us in no doubt about the omnipotence of our Creator. But in choosing us to be his representatives, he allows us to demonstrate his loving power as we engage with the responsibility of extending his kingdom. Our power comes from the presence of the Holy Spirit in our lives, and we can only exercise it by humbly submitting our lives to him. As we learn to be led by the Spirit, and welcome his manifest presence, we become channels for his powerful ministry. Power always emanates from authority – God authorizes us to exercise power on his behalf.

As disciples of Jesus we have a responsibility to represent the King and his kingdom. He gives us his authority and power to do this. Kingdom authority and kingdom power are to be part of the normal Christian life. In fact, representing the King means learning to function with the authority and power he bestows upon us.

A Kingdom Perspective on Prophecy

How does a well-developed and active understanding of kingdom responsibility influence our approach to prophetic ministry? I want to reiterate that kingdom impetus must always flow from a covenant mindset. So our motivation to represent the King and speak out his words of truth and freedom must come from an overwhelming encounter with the Father's heart. It's also worth pointing out that there is a lot of overlap with the themes of 'covenant' and 'kingdom' when we look at the subject of prophecy. But it's vital to make time to focus on the kingdom aspect of the prophetic, in order to sharpen our ministry and bring much-needed balance.

The kingdom perspective brings a necessary **outward momentum** to prophecy. There is a temptation for prophetic people to be quite content remaining in our prayer closets and worship services – those cosy prophetic environments – happily pouring out our love and adoration to God, enjoying his presence. This is all well and good, apart from the obvious lack of engagement with the world around us. Whereas a covenant attitude is all about stepping back, and resting in God's love, a kingdom perspective brings motivation to step out in the prophetic. It makes prophecy active, dynamic and forward moving. Revelation is not only to be enjoyed as part of our relationship with our Father, but it gives us an urgency to be about the business of the King and to be sent out by him.

A kingdom approach brings great **balance** to prophetic ministry – yes, we pursue God's presence, but we are then sent out to represent the One who loves us. 'Kingdom' is about responsibility, and it's important for prophetic people to fully embrace the idea of responsibility. What are we going to do with all that God has put in us? He has poured out his gifts upon us, and given us his Spirit. How are we going to give him a good return on his investment?

Every disciple who can hear the Shepherd's voice has a responsibility:

- to **release** the King's words of life to people
- to **represent** the King and his kingdom through prophetic actions
- to **realign** hearts and minds to the kingdom of God

Each of these facets of kingdom prophecy has a strong missional element to it. We know that prophecy is not simply a gift for the church, but a gift for the world as well. As we've seen throughout this book, a prophetic lifestyle is one with a robust outward dimension. These three 'R's' are about extending the kingdom – both inside and outside the church. All three are also about **encounter** – enabling people to encounter the presence of God and the reality of his kingdom as we practice simple obedience in prophetic words and deeds.

Let's look in more detail at each one:

1. Release: speaking kingdom words

> "The Spirit of the Lord is on me, because he has anointed me to proclaim good news to the poor..."
> Luke 4:18

According to Jesus, one of the signs of the kingdom is the anointed 'speaking out' of good news to those who really need to hear it.

The Bible talks about the power of the tongue, both to bless and to curse. The book of Proverbs tells us that, the soothing tongue is a tree of life, but a perverse tongue crushes the spirit (15:4), and that the words of the reckless pierce like swords, but the tongue of the wise brings healing (12:18). We do well to heed the wisdom of Proverbs 18:21 which warns us that the tongue has the power of life and death.

Prophetic people, walking in the power of the Spirit, can be expectant of the potency of the God-given words they speak.

So often the words spoken by the world around us are negative and destructive. As representatives of the King we are called to advance his kingdom and push back the powers of darkness. As prophetic people we can do this by hearing God's voice and then speaking out words of truth, hope, life, freedom and beauty. We channel his living word to those who need to hear it. We speak the substance of heaven.

The kingdom of God is about God's light coming into dark places. We can be channels of God's light by something as simple as speaking out a word that comes straight from God's heart. It's good to remember that prophecy has the potential to be a supernatural sign that points people to Jesus. In my church we love taking prophecy to the streets and asking the Holy Spirit to show us who is ready to hear a word of life from the Father. I love these encounters and seeing the power of prophetic words in reaching out to those who don't yet know Jesus. Good news is a struggling single mum hearing God's tender affirmation of her parenting skills. Good news is a newly engaged couple hearing that God wants to bless their marriage. Good news is a depressed man hearing the reality of God's love for him.

As representatives of the King he gives us **authority** to speak his words of truth and life. He calls us to become 'speakers of life'. We can have confidence because we speak with the authority he gives us, the authority of the King. And we can expect our prophetic words to carry **power** – power to set the captives free and bring sight to the spiritually blind.

Whether we are on the streets or in the church we can take hold of the gift of prophecy as an effective tool and weapon to advance the kingdom and set people free. There is something significant in knowing that you are a representative of God's kingdom when you speak out prophetic words over people and over circumstances. Every one of us can prophesy in a way that releases the reality of the kingdom into people's lives.

2. Represent: demonstrating the kingdom

A kingdom perspective on prophecy is also about representing the King through prophetic actions and lifestyle. As I said in Chapter 3, prophecy doesn't always have to involve words. Sometimes being prophetic means we are called to demonstrate the kingdom of God through the way we live our lives.

This is about the kingdom responsibility of **embodying the message**.

If we are carriers of a prophetic message then we need to consider to what extent we are called to incarnationally live out this message ourselves. Sometimes actions do indeed speak louder than words.

For example, a number of years ago God began to speak to our church in Sheffield about living in extended 'families on mission'. These are households made up of all sorts of different people – young, old, families, singles – with a shared missional focus. There were a number of prophetic people who stepped out in faith and chose to live the message. Very few others were doing this at the time, but this small group of people chose to be forerunners. Years later our church now has many of these missional households, but I believe the spiritual breakthrough came because of the small number of people who chose to sacrificially embody the original message.

We see a similar model with some of the Old Testament prophets for whom a prophetic ministry meant being much more than God's spokesperson. Hosea's family life was a prophetic symbol used to convey God's prophetic word to his people (Hosea 1:2-11). Jeremiah was also called to embody God's message, through prophetic actions (13:1-11; 32:6-15) or the circumstances of his life (16:1-4).

Prophets, whether old or new covenant, come in all different shapes and sizes, and there is one particular sub-set that I like to refer to as the 'Signs Prophets'. For these people, their life is a sign – a prophetic message. From a worldly perspective they are the ones who go around doing strange things, such as lying prostrate in the middle of the city centre for an hour, or banging huge sticks on the floor throughout worship services. Of all the different varieties of prophets, these are the ones who ruffle the most feathers – and often have to face the greatest levels of rejection. We need to be careful not to judge them, though, because in my experience many of them are simply walking in radical obedience to Jesus and we need to pay close attention to the prophetic word they are embodying.

Even if there is not a specific prophetic message that we are called to demonstrate, there is the broader picture of how we live a prophetic lifestyle through actively representing God's kingdom in this world. As I look around at my prophetic friends, the ones I most want to imitate and follow are not necessarily the ones who can tell me what I had for breakfast yesterday, but those who are so committed to following Jesus wherever he leads them, that their whole life is a beautiful prophetic picture: the King is revealed to everyone who meets them.

3. Realign: seeing the kingdom

In this section I want to focus some more on the spiritual dimension of the kingdom of God – and the fact that the physical world around us is not the only reality.

The Bible speaks to us of two worlds: the physical, material world and the spiritual world. When we look at the life of Jesus we see how he lived from the perspective of the spiritual dimension while at the same time fully engaging with the physical world around him. As he walked this earth the two worlds collided as the kingdom of heaven frequently broke into our world: the supernatural met the natural. As disciples of Jesus we too need to live in, and engage with, both these realities.

The kingdom of God is very real but so much of it is unseen to physical eyes because it is not of the material world. Jesus declared to Pilate, *"My kingdom is not of this world."* (John 18:36) To perceive it requires eyes of faith and expectancy. Part of our role as kingdom people is to see the spiritual dimension of the kingdom in order to demonstrate it and reveal it in the world we live in.

There is an interesting story in 2 Kings 6. The king of Aram had sent a strong military force to capture Elisha who was residing in the city of Dothan. When Elisha's servant got up early one morning he saw an Aramean army of horses and chariots surrounding the city, and was understandably fearful. *"Oh, my lord, what shall we do?"* he asked the prophet. Elisha responded to the servant's alarm by reassuring him that, *"those who are with us are more than those who are with them,"* and then went on to pray a very significant prayer:

> *"Open his eyes, Lord, so that he may see."*
> *Then the Lord opened the servant's eyes, and he looked and saw the hills full of horses and chariots of fire all around Elisha.*
> 2 Kings 6:17

Elisha knew that despite the evidence apparent in the physical world there was another reality: the unseen reality of the heavenly hosts that were protecting him that day. This is where he chose to fix his attention.

In the New Testament Paul writes about where our focus needs to be:

> *So we fix our eyes not on what is seen, but on what is unseen, since what is seen is temporary, but what is unseen is eternal.*
> 2 Corinthians 4:18

> *Since, then, you have been raised with Christ, set your hearts on things above, where Christ is, seated at the right hand of God.*
> Colossians 3:1

This is a call to lavish our attention on the spiritual, the unseen realm of the kingdom of heaven; to not be so caught up in the material reality around us that we fail to perceive this other reality. We can only do this by faith, knowing that the spiritual realm is as real as the physical world:

> *Now faith is confidence in what we hope for and assurance about what we do not see.*
> Hebrews 11:1

Faith is what brings the realities of the kingdom into the world around us. Faith is the lens through which we can see the unseen.

Prophetic people have a great role to play in helping the rest of the church see the reality of the kingdom, so that hearts and minds can be **realigned** to God's purposes. One sub-set of prophets who are particularly good at this are the 'Seers'. They move primarily in the realm of dreams and visions and have the fascinating ministry of awakening the church to the realities of the spiritual realm. Biblical examples are people like Ezekial and Zechariah, both of whom had a series of incredible visions. And then, of course, there is the apostle John, whose book of Revelation contains profound perspectives on God's throne, the sovereignty of Jesus, and angelic activity. I personally know a number of godly seer prophets and find it's always worthwhile listening to them as they describe their recent prophetic experiences. Their heavenly perspective on current events and circumstances builds my faith and motivates me to pray.

Even if we are not all seers, we can still actively seek a kingdom perspective. We can look to see the signs of the kingdom around us, even if they are as small as a mustard seed. Jesus proclaimed that the kingdom of God is at hand (Mark 1:15). God's reality is closer than we can imagine, it's right in front of us, we simply need eyes of faith to see it.

The apostle Paul reminds us that *our citizenship is in heaven,* (Philippians 3:20) and as citizens of heaven we can ask God for a heavenly – a kingdom – perspective. We can regularly ask:

Where is God at work?

Where is the kingdom breaking out?

As we start to get answers to these questions, we can then make sure we're fully aligned with the kingdom; that our plans and strategies are in line with heaven's. Jesus gives us a great model for this. He told his disciples that he only did what he **saw** the Father doing (John 5:19). That was Jesus' strategy for ministry: to see what his heavenly Father was already doing, and then join in.

A kingdom perspective on prophetic ministry involves choosing to see things as God sees them. This is especially true in our dealings with other people: we train ourselves to see God at work them. A kingdom mindset is one that chooses to look at people and see their kingdom potential, and then call it out with authority. Prophecy is birthed in heaven, and when we prophesy over a person we are declaring heaven's perspective over their lives. The gift of prophecy can be used very effectively to align people with God's purposes for them and empower them to step out into their calling.

Stepping Out in Faith

In the previous chapter I wrote about how the number one key to growing in prophecy is to spend time in God's presence. Covenant relationship always comes before kingdom responsibility. There are no shortcuts to a deep relationship with God, cultivated over many years, and this will always be the life source of prophecy and hearing his voice. However the kingdom side to growing in the prophetic is realising our responsibilities and stepping out in faith. If we want to grow in the prophetic we should seek every opportunity to put the gift of prophecy into practice and thus invest in the lives of others.

I believe that the Parable of the Talents in Matthew 25 has much to say to us about how we can all grow in the prophetic, because it speaks of the principle of putting our gifts to work, so we can give God a good return on his investment:

> Again, it will be like a man going on a journey, who called his servants and entrusted his wealth to them. To one he gave five talents of money, to another two talents, and to another one talent, each according to his ability. Then he went on his journey. The man who had received the five talents went at once and put his money to work and gained five more. So also, the one with the two talents gained two more. But the man who had received one talent went off, dug a hole in the ground and hid his master's money.

We all know what happened: the men who had carefully invested what they were given were put in charge of many things and received the blessing of their master. But the servant who hid the money in the ground was cursed, and the small amount he had was taken off him.

This parable exhorts us to use what we've got and to invest it wisely and expectantly. Jesus says that if we are faithful in a little we will be given much. The invitation is to take what you've got and use it, even if it's really little.

Are you being faithful with the level of prophetic insight and revelation you currently have?

Some of us wait a lifetime to receive what we consider to be a reasonable level of 'anointing', but it's the people who are prepared to step out in faith with the smallest level of prophetic proficiency that will see the greatest return on their investment. A kingdom mindset is one that carefully considers how to be faithful with whatever investment God has put within us. I'm always incredibly challenged by the people I know who, with grateful hearts, put whatever gift God has given them to work with utter determination.

I think two of the most powerful words we can say to God are, "*I'm available*". When we choose to step out in a little, God always gives us more. And the more frequently we practice using the gift, the quicker we will grow in confidence and accuracy.

If you are learning how to operate in the gift of prophecy, then you have at your disposal a fantastic opportunity for kingdom purposes. Your daily question can be:

How can I advance God's kingdom with this gift he has given me?

Growing in Kingdom-Focused Prophecy

A balanced prophetic ministry is one that both draws people deeper into their covenant identity **and** empowers them to engage with the kingdom of God. When we prophesy over people we should be eager for words that ignite and sustain forward momentum, that catalyse God's people into action, and that empower them to embrace their calling. This might look like:

- speaking words of future purpose
- giving directional words that shape vision
- sharing prophecies that equip people to do the things Jesus did
- encouraging people to step out in faith
- enabling people to connect with God's missional heart

I'm going to finish this chapter with a testimony from my friend Heather who has used the gift of prophecy to extend the kingdom of light into some dark places.

I was never someone who felt comfortable with traditional forms of evangelism. Handing out tracts or going door-to-door could make me feel physically sick but sometimes guilt would overtake the sickness and I would force myself to do it anyway. Somewhere, in the depth of my being, there was always the thought that it wasn't supposed to be like this! Then in 2002 I started taking courses written by John Paul Jackson on prophecy. John Paul would tell stories of teams that he had trained that have gone to festivals like 'Burning Man' and the 'Sundance' film festival where people would have the most amazing encounters with God. The more stories he told the more a fire started burning in my spirit. This seemed like a form of evangelism I could do.

Since then I have found myself in places I could never have imagined. A few years ago I was asked to be part of a Christian team that was going in to the 'Mind, Body, Spirit' festival in London. This is the largest New Age event in Europe and regularly sees over 20,000 people through the doors over the May Bank Holiday weekend. We were allocated a very small space that we decorated simply, by having white voile covering the sides and back of our booth. We had a set of star lights coming down the back wall and a wooden bowl with white fairy lights on the table. The table was covered with a plain white tablecloth. We were giving out the message that we were there to bring light into the event. As there is always a variety of spiritual influences at work in these arenas we were very careful to have a large team of intercessors providing prayer cover for us all. It was interesting to note just how many of our 'clients' said that they felt drawn to our space and were aware of the lightness and peace that we carried.

At this event we could not openly advertise that we were offering Christian prophetic ministry. This was because the organisers would expect us to be registered with the British Psychic Society, which we did not want to do. Instead we called ourselves 'Spirit Dream Team' and concentrated on telling people we would interpret their dreams (using the same method as Joseph and Daniel in the Old Testament:

interpretation belongs to God). We also offered 'Healing Prayers' and 'Spiritual Encounters'. Through this ministry we saw many of our clients make significant steps closer to God.

One woman came to us telling of recurring dreams in which she was to marry a man that she did not recognise. She wanted us to tell her who this man was. As a team of three, we were all aware of God revealing to us that the man in the dream was Jesus, but none of us felt that he was giving us the green light to share this with the woman initially. So we explained that we felt that these dreams were a message from God and that as she was so intent on getting an answer, perhaps she should ask him directly. We encouraged the woman to close her eyes and to quietly and calmly ask him the question.

After a few minutes the woman opened her eyes and we asked her to tell us what, if anything, had happened. She then went on to describe how she felt someone take her by the hand and she then went flying with this person through outer space. The person told her that he had created the stars and that he loved her. She referred to this person as 'The Prince of the Universe'. So we talked to her about how this Prince came to earth 2000 years ago and lived among people in the Middle East, but some people didn't like him and arranged for him to be killed on a cross. At this point the woman said, "That sounds like Jesus, is it Jesus?" and we said, "Yes". Her response was "When I was flying through space I kept hearing the name 'Jesus' but I didn't want it to be Jesus". As she told us more about her background, it turned out that she had been brought up in a strict Catholic family and that her concept of who Jesus is was negatively coloured by what she had been told as she was growing up. If we had jumped in and told her Jesus was the man in her dreams from the start then she would have rejected the idea. However, because we were obedient to God and had allowed him to 'do his thing' she was many steps closer to entering his kingdom.

Chapter 13

Doing Prophecy Well

I've had the privilege of working alongside some amazing people over the years, and leading some incredibly gifted prophets. For many of these people the prophetic is something that comes very easily to them: they've 'just known' things for as long as they can remember. Such people regularly experience vibrant and dynamic revelation and they see and hear things of the Spirit with remarkable clarity. It's almost as if their spiritual antennae are larger and more sensitive than everyone else's.

I'm really thankful that for some people it is that easy – for one thing they remind me that there is always so much more to receive in the way of revelation from our generous Father. However, my heart has always been for those of us who find it more of a struggle to tune into God's voice, for the sheep in the flock who need a little help with hearing the Good Shepherd. And I know that in order to develop and build a thriving prophetic culture in **any** church we have to find an approach to prophecy that is inclusive, where everyone can join in. We have to make prophecy normal and accessible.

There is a fantastic prize at stake: a church culture where everyone is confident in hearing God's voice for themselves, where the gift of prophecy is part of everyone's spiritual toolkit, where prophetic people are effectively discipled and released to be a blessing, where people have individual and corporate vision for what God's called them to, and where prophecy is taken outside the church walls and into the world. But how do we get there? How do we navigate our way past all the hazards: the misunderstandings, the controversy and the fear that so often accompany prophetic ministry?

My hope and prayer is that in reading this book up to this point you will have a growing vision for the huge potential that a prophetic culture has to offer the church and the world. Prophecy is great! It's one of the most important gifts God has given his church. And it is certainly within reach of **every** church to develop a healthy and mature prophetic culture. So what I want to do in this final chapter is to look at how we can do things really well – with excellence and intention.

It is really important to get it right and do it well, because, whether we like it or not, prophetic ministry is always going to draw detractors, and the enemy will do all he can to twist and distort the flow of pure revelation. Prophecy is a powerful supernatural gift and it is very easy to get off track. We've all heard horror stories, we've all seen unaccountable people using the gift in ways they shouldn't have. People have been hurt and damaged by the immature and insecure handling of prophetic ministry. Because the enemy knows the huge potential for good that accompanies this gift, he comes and does all he can in his power to warp and twist it, and to counterfeit it.

One of the main challenges I've faced in leading prophetic ministry in a large church for a number of years is that of walking a fine line: on the one hand I want to release as many people as possible into the prophetic, but I also want to keep it really safe so that nobody gets damaged in any way by the ministry. The aim is for an 'orderly freedom,' that functions in such a way that it promotes unity and common understanding, and has a biblical foundation.

There is a great need for a ministry of real integrity, while realising that mistakes are an inevitable part of growing in the prophetic. Prophetic people *will* make mistakes – but that doesn't mean we should shut down their ministry. Let's face it, we would never stop someone from preaching after one bad sermon, and yet there is often a lot less grace shown to prophets who miss the mark. We need a culture where we can be honest and open about the times we get things wrong, while ensuring that people are protected from the consequences of poor prophecy.

We've seen how the theology of 'covenant and kingdom' provides the foundation for our approach to prophetic ministry. Let's now go on to consider some **key values** that will do much to shape a healthy prophetic culture. If we get these values in place then we're going to be safe, and the people we're ministering to are going to be safe. It is then within reach of every mainstream, biblical church to grow a culture where it is normal to hear God, and to make it really easy and accessible for people to join in.

Values for a Healthy Prophetic Culture

The values and principles, which provide a firm basis for a healthy prophetic culture, are encapsulated in three words: **holistic**, **grounded** and **multipliable**. We've already met many of these key values; what I'm doing in this section is drawing them all together.

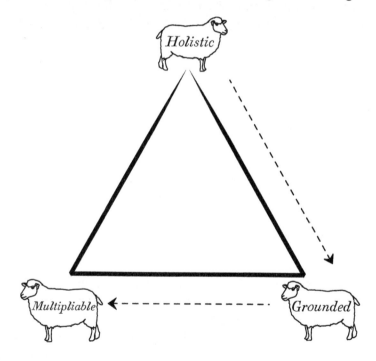

- Holistic

    "Characterized by the belief that the parts of something are intimately interconnected and explicable only by reference to the whole."
    Oxford English Dictionary

A multi-faceted approach

In a holistic prophetic culture there is an understanding that we can hear God speak through many spiritual disciplines and practices, rather than 'one size fits all'. Many streams and expressions of worship, and different ways of doing church, are embraced. It's surprising how easy it is to make assumptions about how to create a 'prophetic atmosphere' but we need to recognise that loud charismatic worship isn't the only way to create an environment for engaging with the prophetic.

As we saw in Chapter 2, we all hear God in different ways: some in the quiet of an empty room; some in the middle of a worship service; some in the stepping out of day-to-day life. And the form the revelation takes will be different: some people hear God through words, some through prophetic pictures, some through a 'just knowing'. It's important to communicate and model that all forms of revelation are equally legitimate.

There are many different expressions of Spirit-breathed revelation, and we need to recognise that someone baking a cake for a friend in need in direct response to the Holy Spirit, is as valid as the person standing at the front of church on Sunday delivering a prophecy.

Balance

To grow a holistic prophetic culture, both Word and Spirit need to be encompassed, so that there is healthy engagement with both the Bible and the Holy Spirit. People need to understand how the two interact with each other and how we should grow in engagement with both of them.

There is a great benefit to having prophets and teachers working together. Acts 13:1 tells us that *in the church at Antioch there were prophets and teachers* – which is a great reminder of how profitable it is when both ministries can work alongside each other. The more powerful and prominent prophetic ministry grows in our churches, the more important good biblical teaching becomes, so that we can base everything in scripture and not be led astray. The two ministries have different functions, but they really need each other. The prophets' perspective is: *"This is what God is saying"*; the teachers' response is: *"This is what scripture says about it"*. We need a healthy balance between the two.

So it's important as we build a prophetic culture to have good links with the teachers and invite them into the process. An immature prophetic ministry will distance itself from them, but a mature one says, *"Come alongside us on this journey and keep us faithful to scripture."*

We also need to ensure that within the output of prophetic ministry there is a balance of invitation and challenge, and that prophetic people understand that the Holy Spirit brings both of these. As people first learn how to use the gift of prophecy it is usually the case that most of the words they give will be of simple encouragement, and therefore very invitational. But in a mature prophetic culture there is openness to the Holy Spirit bringing words of healthy challenge and refinement.

Different settings

A really holistic prophetic culture is one where prophecy operates well in a variety of different settings: Sunday services, small groups, missional communities and every place where people are coming together. Prophecy is a gift for both the centre and the edge of church community. It's a mistake to create the sort of culture where people only experience prophetic ministry in the 'professional' setting of large gathered church, because it can easily give the impression that prophecy is best left to the senior leaders and those specially anointed people. In fact the most fruitful place for people to grow in using the gift is definitely not Sunday services, rather it's in the smaller and more informal context provided by places like house groups.

• Grounded

Grounded in discipleship and accountability

We've already looked at how important it is to root the prophetic in a strong culture of discipleship and accountability, where everyone knows that their primary calling and identity is that of a disciple.

The big picture we need to get hold of is of a prophetic culture *within* a culture of discipleship and mission. A strong discipleship culture will automatically bring in accountability.

Grounded in community

It's important that as we grow the prophetic in our churches we intentionally avoid a consumer model of prophetic ministry. And by that I mean where people have the attitude, *"In order to hear God speak to me I have to go and find a prophet ..."* We need to work hard to ensure the prophetic ministry in our churches is not focused on a few gifted individuals, the 'celebrity' prophets. There is a danger of one or two people becoming the only channels of God's voice in a church, and people end up looking to them as the connection to God, rather than pursuing their own relationship with the Lord. In our church here in Sheffield there are some amazingly anointed prophetic people but we have to watch and be careful that we don't end up with a little gaggle of people following them round on a Sunday morning saying, *"Please prophesy over me!"* We can all learn to use the gift; it must never become an exclusive ministry.

Prophetic ministry that is grounded in community will counteract the consumer tendencies inherent in society, because the focus naturally shifts to the community hearing God together, rather than it all being about a few individuals. The more we practice listening to God together, in our local expressions of church, the more we will take on the identity of the flock of Jesus hearing him corporately, with everyone having a valid contribution to make.

A strong focus on community keeps prophecy grounded because it brings with it the vision of the body made up of many necessary parts and a diversified team ministry:

> *From him the whole body, joined and held together by every supporting ligament, grows and builds itself up in love, as each part does its work.*
> Ephesians 4:16

In fact a mature prophetic ministry is one that is refined and shaped by the other five-fold ministries and takes great joy in working alongside them.

A thriving Christian community is one made up of all ages, and one of the best ways to grow a healthy prophetic culture is to release the children and teach them how to prophesy. In fact kids generally find it much easier to hear God's voice because they tend to have much less emotional 'baggage' to get in the way. We recently had all the children praying and prophesying over the adults at the end of a Sunday service, which was a blessing to all concerned, and a great picture of community coming together to engage with God.

Grounded in love and humility

It should be no surprise to us that right in the middle of Paul's teaching on spiritual gifts, in his first letter to the Corinthians, is his great hymn to love. I never fail to be moved and challenged by 1 Corinthians 13. It has the power to strip away all the pretension and self-importance that so often entangles prophetic ministry. Prophecy without love is no more than a *clanging cymbal*. We can only pursue the gift of prophecy to the extent that we *follow the way of love* (1 Corinthians 14:1).

And the further we go in prophecy, the more we have to have humble hearts. Moses is a great example for us: the man who was more humble than anyone else was the man who met God face-to-face. Pride is so corrosive and it can get in very subtly. But there is no room for pride in prophetic ministry. When we prophesy God alone is to be exalted. Humility is about laying down every one of our own agendas so we can dwell in the place of God's agenda.

Grounded in reality: understanding event and process

As we've seen, the prophetic process doesn't stop at revelation; we have to consider the **outworking** of God's word to us. This is about making it real: allowing prophecy to become flesh, so that it takes root and bears fruit and edifies the church community. This is where the prophetic really benefits from working closely with the apostolic. The prophet is focused on the question, *"What is God saying?"* The apostle asks, *"What's the best way to see the thing that God wants to do established?"*

A prophetic culture without the apostolic will ultimately be weak and ineffective; focused on vision but lacking the application, and losing its missional momentum. There is a real cost for the prophet to fully embrace the ministry of the apostles – but we need to do this in order to build a grounded prophetic ministry.

- ## Multipliable

One of the things that excites me most about a mature prophetic culture is that it is multipliable: it reproduces itself.

Demystifying the prophetic

In order to produce a culture of multiplication we first of all have to demystify the prophetic and make it accessible for everyone. We need to be careful and disciplined with our use of language so that it doesn't alienate people through 'super-spiritual' jargon. When Jesus taught his followers about hearing his voice he used the normal, everyday picture of a shepherd and sheep. We too have to learn to use accessible language that conveys the message, through the words we use, that anyone can hear God.

Imitation

We learn by watching – by seeing how other people do it. To effectively multiply prophetic ministry we need to do it in such a way so that others can imitate us. We have to give people a framework to climb on. So this means not just doing ministry at the front of church, but being close enough to people so that they can see how it works in our lives on a day-to-day basis. It means inviting people to come and join in with us.

Leaders are the ones who really set culture, and so they are the ones who need to model it. If you want to see a healthy, mature prophetic culture grow in your church, be prepared to model it well. Convey the message that, *"We value prophecy, we want it, and we exercise it ourselves,"* through testimonies, teaching and example.

Focus on investing in others and multiplying ourselves

There can be a lot of navel-gazing in prophetic circles, but to grow a healthy prophetic culture the focus needs to shift from ourselves and the question, *"How can we get even better at this?"* to, *"How can we invest in other people so that they can do what we do?"*

In order to empower every member of the church to hear God we need to remember Jesus' story of the seed that goes into the ground and dies in order to produce a harvest (John 12:24). There is a sacrificial element to investing in others, and this is particularly pertinent for prophets, who are happy alone in their prayer closets.

The ultimate aim for any prophet has to be to raise up people who are more prophetic than them. It should never be about 'my' ministry, but about the ministry of Jesus being multiplied into as many lives as possible.

The multiplication of ourselves is the essence of leadership. Looking at what Jesus did should give us great hope:

- he was able to take a group of twelve people, invest in them, and teach them to do all that he could do in less than three years
- he multiplied his life into theirs
- he gave his disciples complete access to his life so that they could imitate him and then in turn become little 'Jesus's.'

To follow the model set for us by Jesus, and multiply our life and ministry into others, means having people close enough to us so that we can properly invest in them. A regular question to be asking the Lord is, *"Who do you want me to invest in, in this season?"*

Reproducible and scalable

To grow a prophetic ministry that is accessible to everyone we have to provide people with reproducible and scalable patterns of ministry, easy ways to start engaging with prophecy.

I love collecting many different prophetic 'activation' exercises: these are group exercises that train people in how to hear God's voice. They are easy to learn and easy to pass on to others, and work in different social spaces. Multiplication of ministry happens when everyone feels empowered to teach another person a simple way to hear God's voice.[13]

A Culture of Expectancy

To grow a thriving and effective prophetic culture it's important that we become expectant and confident that God will speak to us if we ask him to. This is not about a few faith-filled individuals, but about a community that expects to hear God's voice. It's about a corporate

....

[13] You will find many activation exercises in *The Prophecy Course*, published by 3DM

attitude of expectancy. Too often the reason we are not seeing the kingdom of God break out in our midst with signs and wonders is because we're not actually expecting God to do much, and we're certainly not putting ourselves in the place where we really need God to speak. As Graham Cooke writes, *"Expectancy is the lifeblood of moving in the Spirit."*[14]

We're familiar with Paul's exhortation to *eagerly desire gifts of the Spirit, especially prophecy* (1 Corinthians 14:1), but what does this really look like in the context of church community? How do we go about corporately pursuing prophecy?

It's all very well believing that the gift of prophecy is available to every believer; we need to become active practitioners. Here are two straightforward ways to develop corporate expectancy, so that it becomes ingrained in our church culture.

• Space

It's often as simple as making space to listen to God. It's surprising how many churches don't provide the space for community listening, and actively engaging together with the Holy Spirit's revelation.

This is about getting in the habit of whenever people are gathered to say, *"Let's just wait on the Lord for a few minutes..."* So at our church this is something we aim to do regularly, whether it's staff prayers, pre-service prayers, or leadership meetings.

In the 3DM Europe office we aim to start every team meeting with a short time of prayer and then a short time of listening, and we are getting so blessed by the revelation God is bringing to us as we engage with this simple discipline. We are learning the habit of listening before talking.

• Opportunity

One of the best ways of growing prophetic culture in our churches is to give lots of opportunities for people to step out in faith and have a go. This is actually pretty straightforward: we simply teach people the

---

[14] Graham Cooke - *Approaching the Heart of Prophecy* (Vancouver: Brilliant Book House, 2010), 121

basics of how to hear God and then say, *"Off you go – go and do it – here are some people to practice on..."*

We need to develop a culture where it's safe and normal to have a go, and where people have freedom to fail. In order for people to grow in prophetic gifts they need to be able to step out and take risks – without fear of rejection or condemnation if they get it wrong. So we provide them with a safe and releasing environment, with lots of grace and patience for mistakes.

In any church there are plenty of opportunities to practise prophecy. In my role here in Sheffield I am always on the look out to provide practise space for people I have trained up. So whether it's business leaders, families, couples about to be married, a particular missional community, or the leadership team, there will always be an opportunity somewhere for people to practise exercising the gift of prophecy.

The more people practise, the more they will grow in confidence, and the more testimonies there will be to encourage the church and raise the level of expectancy all God's children can learn to use this wonderful gift.

Parameters

To do prophecy well we need to provide clearly defined parameters. This is not about restricting the leading of the Holy Spirit, or quenching the anointing, but it is about providing a safe context so that prophetic ministry can flourish with the full blessing of the church community. Clear guidelines for ministry, which are then openly communicated and owned by the church, are vital.

Why do we need guidelines and boundaries?

- it's a way to release the learners, because when people are first stepping out in the gift they will feel reassured by the presence of simple parameters which help them focus on what is expected of them

- they give recipients a sense of security: it's really important that people feel safe when they are receiving prophetic ministry

- discipline is good for prophetic people! A mature prophet is someone who really welcomes guidelines, because it shows that they have the best interests of the whole church at heart

I would encourage you to put together agreed guidelines and protocol for prophetic ministry in your church, and then let the leaders, the prophets and the rest of the church know what these are. Each church context, and set of parameters, will be different, but here are some of the more generic guidelines that we use in a public setting here in Sheffield:

- Always minister in pairs. Mixed pairs can prophesy over men or women, but ideally two women should only prophesy over women, and vice-versa.
- All prophetic words must be recorded.
- Avoid very directional words (these are prophecies that would significantly affect the direction of someone's life, for example, *"God is calling you to China!"*)
- Do not give the **application** of a prophecy, i.e. don't tell the recipient what they should do in response to the prophecy you give them.
- Do not prophesy future babies or marriages.

These are the types of guidelines we use with prophetic ministry teams in a public context. We also have a policy of not allowing an 'open mic' in our main Sunday services, i.e. if someone wants to share a prophecy from the front of church they always have to privately submit it to the service leader first, who will weigh it and discern the best thing to do with it. There have been plenty of times when I have not been released to share a word publicly, and I think that's a really good thing! The last thing I want is for the service leaders to feel under any pressure to give the well-known prophet a platform. I'm also very keen to model submission to leadership to everyone in the congregation.

I want to make it clear that our guidelines are context specific – things will look different in missional communities and small groups. So, for example, I wouldn't expect the guideline about ministering in pairs to be followed in the context of a small group where everyone knows and trusts each other.

Having a clear set of guidelines and protocol then makes it much easier to train people in prophetic ministry.

How to Prophesy Well

The art of prophesying well is something we can all cultivate. Good practice will make all the difference to how prophecy is perceived and received in our churches. This may look like a long and comprehensive list, but the more we practise the more natural it will all become:

- Start in a place of rest. Examine your heart for any sense of striving. Remember, we can't manufacture prophecies; it's up to God. Our job is to simply listen with faith. If you detect that you are striving, then take a while to step back into your covenant identity and rest in the Father's love. Prophecy born out of striving will be of limited value.

- Don't allow frustration and pressure to hear God get in the way. As we see in the life of Elijah, God's voice is found in the stillness rather than the storm. Psalm 46:10 teaches us to *be still and know that I am God.* Beware of speaking when your spirit is uneasy, you are in turmoil, or you feel forced to speak.

- Don't be influenced by what you see with your physical eyes: we can be easily prejudiced by visual information. It's all too easy to make false assumptions. For example, if the person in front of us is looking upset, we may assume they need a word of comfort from God, but the Holy Spirit may have other plans. So instead we must focus on revelation from the Spirit. It's important to walk by faith and not by natural senses or feelings.

- Ask God to fill your heart with his love for the people or person you are ministering to (1 Corinthians 14:1). Desire to serve them. Be hungry for words which will strengthen, encourage and comfort them (1 Corinthians 14:3). Imagine yourself as a channel of love coming straight out of the Father's heart.

- Actively lay down your own agendas, any preconceived ideas, your reason, your own understanding (Proverbs 3:5). Surrender them all to the Lord.

- Ask God questions. Ask him for his perspective. What does he see? What words of encouragement does he want to release in this situation? What aspect of his nature does he want to reveal? What is the Spirit doing here?

- As God starts to speak to you, don't be tempted to dismiss things that don't make sense; instead let the Holy Spirit take you deeper into the revelation as he unfolds it to you.

- If you have been given a picture or word, ask the Holy Spirit if there is a corresponding passage of scripture that illuminates the revelation you've been given. There may not be, but it's always good to ask, and it's a good way of bringing confirmation.

- Remember that every prophecy is made up of three parts: revelation, interpretation, and application. If you only receive revelation, don't be tempted to add your own interpretation. Don't prophesy application because this needs to be worked out in community. By far the most useful way of delivering a prophecy is if you make explicit which part is revelation and which part is interpretation. Then the recipient can weigh each part separately.

- Use normal, everyday language and don't shout.

- If you are delivering a prophecy in a public setting – for example, at the front of church – it's a good idea to write it down, or rehearse it quietly before you go up to speak.

- Avoid saying, *"Thus says the Lord!"* Not only is this archaic language, but it leaves no room for weighing. We should speak prophecies in a way that reflects the fact that they all need to be weighed and give the recipients the freedom to weigh (and reject) what they are hearing. A much better way to introduce a prophecy is, *"I think God may be saying something like this…"*

- Don't give someone a word that is highly directional, or corrective, without checking it with your leaders first.

- Make sure that the prophecy is recorded in some way. God's word is very precious but it's amazing how quickly we can forget it. These days most mobile phones have a voice recorder function that makes life very easy (as long as we know how to find it!) When I first started out in prophetic ministry we had to rely on cassette recorders and we were forever running out of tapes!

Afterword

My Sheep Have Ears

Being a follower of Jesus, the Good Shepherd, should be simple rather than complicated. After all sheep are fairly simple creatures. Safe pasture and community are pretty much all they require, and they will happily follow the shepherd they trust.

And for spiritual sheep, the process of learning how to hear the Shepherd's voice should be a simple one: it's as simple as knowing who you are and believing you will hear. Jesus challenged the culture of his day – and continues to challenge our culture – when he said that it's only as we come to him as little children that we will be able to enter his kingdom and know the truth he holds out to us (Matthew 11:25, Luke 18:17). I've heard two stories in the last week of children perceiving the kingdom – through visions of Jesus and of angels – that both thrill me, but also challenge me to beware the blindness that so often accompanies the 'wise and learned'.

I hope and pray that this book has helped you in your journey of learning to hear God's voice, and that for you it will be a simple – child-like and sheep-like – journey from now on. God is speaking, as he has done throughout the whole history of humanity, and he promises us that his sheep will hear his voice.

Accessible Prophecy is a ministry that has grown out of St. Thomas' Church Philadelphia in Sheffield UK (one of the churches in Network Church Sheffield). It is also part of 3DM Europe, an organisation focused on coaching and training Christian leaders who will call, invest in and release disciples to live out the good news of Jesus.

Our vision is to make prophecy normal and accessible. We work with churches to help them develop a healthy prophetic culture, and we work with individuals who desire to grow personally in the gift of prophecy. We provide strategic training, coaching and resources.

For more information please visit our website:

www.accessibleprophecy.com

or contact us at **prophecy@3dmeurope.com**

CPSIA information can be obtained
at www.ICGtesting.com
Printed in the USA
LVOW04s2050281216
519036LV00009B/58/P